All in the
Name of Love

All in the Name of Love

BRUNA MINICOZZI

All in the Name of Love
Bruna Minicozzi

All rights reserved
First Edition, 2023
© Bruna Minicozzi, 2023
Cover image source pexels.com

The author asserts the moral right to be identified as the author of this work.

No part of this publication may be reproduced, distributed, or transmitted in any form or by any means, including photocopying, recording, or other electronic or mechanical methods, without the prior written permission of the author, except in the case of brief quotations embodied in critical reviews and certain other non-commercial uses permitted by copyright law.

Requests for permission should be addressed to
Bruna Minicozzi

ISBN - 978-0-6452486-2-3

Chapter One

The lifelong dream of little girls growing up is to be swept off their feet by a knight in shining armour. To wear a beautiful wedding dress which makes us feel like a princess and to live happily ever after, just like in the fairy tales we have been reading since childhood. But the hardest truth is that fairy tales are just that, fairy tales. It is not that love is not real, but love is rarely unconditional – it is perhaps more aligned with temporary infatuation and momentary lust rather than happily ever after.

My name is Bella. I was born in a tiny town in the south of Italy. I come from humble beginnings and even though we did not have much, we appreciated what we did have. As a child, most of my time was spent with my Nonna as both my parents were working. I was a very strong-willed girl who knew what she wanted. I remember, on one occasion my Nonna had promised me that if I behaved myself and did my chores for a week, she would buy me a pair of boots for Christmas. Keeping her word, she took me shopping the week before Christmas.

As we walked into the shoe store, I saw a pair of red boots that I instantly fell in love with and wanted.

When I showed my Nonna the boots her response was "No I am buying you the black coloured ones". I cried and cried and told her that I didn't want the black ones and that I would not wear them. It was snowing that day and my tears felt like ice on my cheeks.

I was still crying when we reached the bus stop to go home. Here, Nonna pointed out a woman sitting on the bench. She was very poorly dressed, and she had only one leg and the sock and shoe on that leg were full of holes. Nonna whispered to me, "Don't cry. You don't know how lucky you are. You have gloves, a scarf, and a coat to keep you warm and now you also have a nice new pair of boots." But I did not care as I just wanted my red boots. Not until I grew older did I realize the lesson my Nonna was trying to teach me that day.

As I was growing up, my aspirations of what I wanted to be changed on many occasions. First, I wanted to be a schoolteacher, then a hairdresser, a midwife and then I decided I wanted to travel the world.

Chapter Two

My family received a wedding invitation from my aunt in Australia as her daughter and my cousin was getting married. Sabrina and I had grown up together and we were very close. I desperately wanted to go to Australia for the wedding, but my parents simply could not afford my plane fare. I did not know what to do so I wrote to my aunt in Australia asking her to send me a ticket so I could attend the wedding. To my surprise she did. So, at fourteen years of age, I travelled alone to Australia. I arrived in February 1980 for one month. I was excited to meet the members of my family especially my beautiful cousin Sabrina. My aunt handed me a bunch of silk red roses.

The day I arrived in Adelaide my cousin Sabrina took me for a walk around her neighbourhood which was just an excuse so she could sneak out to meet her fiancé as this was not allowed in our culture without the presence of an adult. As we were walking along the footpath a black Cadillac stopped and the gentleman inside asked me for directions. I could not speak English so I turned to Sabrina and she asked him how she could help, to which he again asked for directions then looking my way he said, "Tell her I am going to marry her". I asked Sabrina what he had said as I did not understand. She couldn't stop laughing and said she was going to pee her pants because the man had said that he wanted to marry me. I was confused. I was only 14 years old. Marriage was not something I was thinking about at that age. Later, I found out that he had fallen in love with my blonde long wavy hair and big breasts. He went on his way and I thought he was cute but stupid. I slept in Sabrina's room and we talked and giggled until the wee hours of the morning.

A couple of days later my relatives took me for a drive to Barossa Valley. On another occasion, they took me to the zoo and for the first time I saw a Kangaroo and a Koala. I got to pat the Koalas and it felt like all my Christmases had come at once. We also took a day trip to Wallaroo. We spent the day at the beach and collected a big bucket of cockles. My uncle was very excited but we girls were quite happy to just sit on the beach and enjoy the contents of our picnic basket. My aunt was always trying to fatten me up. I was wearing a bathing suit and she kept telling me to cover my body. On another occasion, we went shopping for clothes. I always had an eye for fashion but I didn't really like the fashion in Australia. Italy was always fashion-forward.

In the evenings we slept on the lawn outside as my aunt didn't have an air-conditioner and it was very hot inside. In the early hours of the morning, one could hear the milkman delivering the milk. Sabrina and I would listen to Abba. We listened constantly to our favourite song "Money Money Money" and knew all the words by heart.

One evening we snuck out so Sabrina could again meet her fiancé. The next morning when we woke up she had a huge love bite on her neck. Luckily, her mother thought something must have bitten her during the night. I didn't even know what it was until Sabrina told me.

My aunt's next-door neighbour was an old lady called Mrs McCain. She was a retired English teacher. She lived in a beautiful large house. Her garden was full of daisies. I can never forget Mrs McCain because she taught me the English language. She tutored me so I could flawlessly deliver my speech on the wedding day. She was so proud of me that evening. She even came and gave me a big hug. We remained friends and she even played the Organ at my wedding. It was an honour to share my special day with her.

Finally, Sabrina's wedding day arrived. I was so excited. I was a bridesmaid for the first time in my life. When we arrived for the reception, to my surprise, I found standing at the door waiting to escort the guests to their seats was the same man who said he wanted to marry me. When he saw me, he screamed with excitement and said, "Here is my angel". Knowing that I did not understand what he was saying, he turned to my cousin, the bride, and asked her to tell me that he was going to ask my dad tonight for my hand in marriage. During the course of the evening, we found out that his name was Antonio. He did not know that he would be speaking to my uncle and not my dad. But he persisted and at the end of the reception, he approached my uncle to ask for my hand in marriage. My uncle told him to come

All in the Name of Love

and see him the next day and then they would have a discussion.

True to his word, Antonio presented himself at my uncle's house the next day. He also brought an interpreter with him as his Italian was not very good. My uncle explained that he was not my father and that I was only 14 years old. Antonio's proposal was out of the question and I would be returning to Italy in two weeks. Then my uncle turned to me and asked if I wanted to marry him, to which I replied, "No, I am too young".

A couple of weeks later I returned to Italy and continued with my life.

Chapter Three

One day I wrote a letter to my teacher explaining that my mum was very ill and I had to take a day off from school. My Nonna signed the note blindly as her vision was impaired. I did this on a regular basis since my return from Australia.

The next morning my best friend Bianca and I both took the day off from school on false pretences and caught a train to Rome to meet with a few boys. We spent an hour or so with them at a museum but very quickly we lost interest in them.

We both worked in an upmarket shop in Rome for a woman named Maria. She was a very distinguished woman with black hair which she pulled back into a slick bun. She was fair but very strict with us. She made sure we sorted the donated goods and displayed them in the most beautiful way possible.

Maria gave us very little money in return for our services, but it was enough as pocket money for us 14-year-old schoolgirls. My mother had always instilled in us that if we wanted money, we had to get a job. My mother raised us to be independent and to stand with dignity on our own two feet.

All in the Name of Love

One Friday afternoon after school, Bianca and I had to sort through a few bags of donated goods. Our eyes were as big as saucers when we realised that the bags were full of Chanel items which included jewellery, long gowns, and a couple of pairs of shorts. I fell in love with a pair of gold embossed shorts so I put them aside to buy them at the end of the week on payday.

We couldn't resist trying on the jewellery. A Chanel necklace which had a pink shoe and a pink lipstick pendant on it caught my eye, so I put it on. Bianca and I were also being silly with the gowns. We were putting them against ourselves and twirling around like two silly young schoolgirls. Just then Maria walked in on us and in a raised voice said, "Come on girls, stop playing around. You are paid to work not to play". She immediately stopped us in our tracks and we got straight back to work.

At the end of the day, Bianca and I caught the train back home as we always did. I went to change out of my best clothes and noticed that the necklace was still around my neck. I was upset and felt very guilty and ashamed. I confessed to my Nonna and began to cry. Nonna felt bad for me as she knew that this was out of character for me and she could see how upset I was. This incident happened just before Easter. Every night we always went to church as a family for lent. That night I left early for church so I could confess to the parish priest. Padre Pietro was very understanding and asked me to stop feeling guilty since it was an innocent mistake. He advised me to return the necklace to Maria and apologise for my error.

The next morning, I was getting ready for school and Nonna was making coffee at the fireplace. She called my name, "Bella, come here". I said, "What have I done now?" and she replied, "You haven't done anything wrong but come here". I slowly walked up to her and she said, "Bella, I am so proud of you and I couldn't ask for a better granddaughter. Close your eyes and put out your hand". I felt something in the palm of my hand and when I opened my eyes, I couldn't believe that my Nonna had given me a five Lire note. I asked Nonna what I had done to deserve this money and she said, 'When you go to work after school, explain to Maria how you panicked when she came to the back of the store the previous day and that is why you forgot to remove the necklace and accidentally left it on. Apologise and offer her the money as payment.'

I did as Nonna had instructed. Maria took the money and said, "It is more than enough to cover the cost of the necklace. Now let's not waste any more time and get back to work". When I finished my shift that night Maria called me over in her usual gruff voice and handed me a bag that she tied up with a double knot and asked me to pass it on to Nonna and tell her that it was from her.

When I returned home that night Nonna had dinner on the table and I told her that Maria had given me a bag for her. Nonna asked me to put it aside and to thank Maria the next day. After dinner as Nonna and I sat by the fire she enquired how my apology had gone that day. I replied, "It was good Nonna, Maria was very understanding". As I was reaching for my Rosary Beads Nonna said, "I am happy for you but when you go to bed tonight don't forget to thank God. The Kingdom of heaven is within you, Bella. Learn to trust your heart when it becomes restless. Never be afraid to speak the truth no matter how bad it may seem. Truth sets you free but lies trap you. Always tell the truth, no matter what happens. You are such an old soul, don't ever change for anyone. People may tell you that you are too young and sometimes people may push you aside as not everybody is going to love you. But remember, the heart goes after what the heart wants as long as you are true to yourself".

Nonna then remembered the bag from Maria. She untied the double knot. Inside was a beautiful black handbag which I have to this day; a yellow silk dress, the Chanel necklace I had worn home by mistake, and the gorgeous, embossed gold shorts. Also, amongst these items was a five Milla Lire note wrapped in a handkerchief. Maria had rewarded me for my honesty and I was grateful for the gifts she had given Nonna and me. Possessions were scarce when I was young as money was always very tight.

Chapter Four

Just after my fifteenth birthday, I resigned from my job in order to pursue my studies. Maria was sad to see me go as I was a hard worker, but she pulled me aside and said, "Bella, if there is anything in the shop that you like, put it aside, and when you leave take them with you". I smiled back at her and thanked her. When I was leaving, I took a beautiful pair of black leather shorts which were very fashionable and I used to wear them at any given opportunity. Maria's gifts became some of my very precious possessions that I ever owned.

So, as a young 15-year-old girl I chased my dreams and boy did I have a blast. I continued my studies and found another part-time job of helping in a hairdressing salon.

One afternoon, a friend of mine and I caught a train to Rome without telling our parents. We were sitting on the Spanish steps when I heard a man's voice say, "There is my angel". I could not believe it when I saw Antonio sitting there. We joined him and his friend and the more I spoke to him the more I realised I was falling for him.

After that day, I tried to spend every moment I could with Antonio, the love of my life. We were so smitten with each other that I would leave school early to spend time with him. One day I told him that I would take a day off from school and spend it with him at the river. My parents had a cellar where they stored surplus food for the winter. I helped myself to some prosciutto and pickled eggplant and I tapped a bottle of wine from the wine barrel. I purchased some fresh bread and packed a picnic basket for the two of us. I was looking forward to spending the day with him. Back then I couldn't be with him on my own so I convinced Bianca to come with me as a chaperone. She came along but didn't stay close to us. She gave us our privacy.

We opened the bottle of wine and Antonio started complimenting me by telling me that I took his breath away with my beauty. I blushed and blurted out, "I am psychic and if you're lying to me, I will be able to pick it up". He put out his hand and said, "Here read my palm, let's see how psychic you are". At that very moment, two musicians came out from behind the huge rocks. One was playing the violin and the other was playing the piano accordion while serenading us. I still remember the song like it was yesterday. Antonio was holding my hand the whole time and it was as if he stole my soul, and at that moment, I fell even more in love with him. I never professed my love to him. I kept it to myself as we had met only for a short time and I couldn't believe how quickly I was falling in love with him.

It was a beautiful autumn day, the feeling of the tenderness of his hand, the sound of water running in the river, and the musicians playing in the background was like a fairy tale. He pulled me close towards him and kissed me passionately. I was experiencing the utmost love for this man as if there was an inferno inside me. At the same time, I was also tormented by the thought that someone might see us together and tell my father.

Later, Antonio and I took a stroll down the river and every time he wanted to hold my hand I pushed it away. I didn't want anyone to see us. But Antonio said, "Bella do you love me?" I replied, "I don't know Antonio". At that moment he grabbed both my hands and said, "I am in love with you Bella, and I will never love another". I replied, "Please give me time, let my heart decide". I was confused as I didn't know how this would end. He was going back to Australia and I didn't want to get hurt.

We met again the next day. He touched my hand and I realised I loved him very much. But we had fallen so quickly in love that I was afraid he wouldn't come back. He convinced me to ask my parents if he could come and speak to them.

I spoke to my father and explained to him how I had met Antonio in Australia and how I liked him very much. My father asked me to invite Antonio for Sunday lunch. I had to tell my father that Antonio's Italian wasn't very good and that his cousin was coming as an interpreter if needed.

My head kept having these crazy thoughts, 'what if my parents didn't like him?' or 'what if my father won't give us his blessings?' I was starting to get worked up so I went for a walk. But I still couldn't get such thoughts out of my head. That Sunday, I nervously got dressed in my best for Antonio's arrival. I was watching out for him from the balcony. I saw him walking towards the house. My heart was beating very fast. He looked so handsome dressed in a white shirt and black trousers. I knew in my heart of hearts that we would grow old together.

Antonio knocked on the front door and my mother greeted him. She invited him in while I just stood there. I looked into his eyes and knew that he was the one for me. I was praying that he would marry me so I could have this euphoric feeling forever. I was so nervous that my mouth was dry and I could barely speak. I said hello to him from a distance, but, I wanted to run over and have him wrap his arms around me and share a passionate kiss. My father approached him and put out his hand for a handshake and I saw that Antonio's hand was trembling.

Dad wished him good morning and asked Antonio what his intentions were regarding me. Antonio replied that he was asking for my hand in marriage. My father paced the floor holding his braces and said, "Why are you asking me, why don't you ask her? She is standing over there. Bella has a mind of her own and I will support her with whatever decision she makes". Antonio walked up to me and asked me if I would marry him. I answered, "Of course, I will!" It wasn't the proposal I had always dreamed of but for now, in front of my parents, it would suffice. I wanted to kiss him there and then, but I couldn't do so in the presence of my parents as it wasn't the respectful thing to do.

My parents asked him to stay for lunch. We had a simple lunch outside under the grape vines with a beautiful view of the valley. During lunch, Antonio explained that he wanted me to come to Australia to be his wife.

Three days before Antonio left for Australia we met secretly at the same spot where he had serenaded me. I was so excited to see him that my heart seemed to be skipping beats. He looked so handsome standing there. I ran into his arms and we hugged each other very hard. Then Antonio was on his knee and he asked for my hand again. He placed a friendship ring on my finger. I didn't know what the ring meant so Antonio explained that it was a ring given as a gift to the one you loved to signify a commitment to each other. It is usually given before an engagement ring. I couldn't share the news about my ring with anyone, I had to keep it to myself.

Soon, it was time for Antonio to go back to Australia. We said our goodbyes and my father and I saw him off at the airport.

Chapter Five

Antonio returned to Australia. I didn't hear from him for two months and it was as if time had frozen. I was so sad and missed him terribly. My sisters were always teasing me saying that he was not coming back. They used to say "Arrivederci Italiana, hello Australiana." These words would get under my skin.

One day I just couldn't get him off my mind. Thousands of questions were going through my head. I decided to go for a long walk to the same spot where Antonio had given me the friendship ring. It was raining so I rugged up, put on my rubber boots, and grabbed an umbrella. I arrived at the spot and sat down on a rock to watch the waterfalls. I started crying, my thoughts heavy. I pulled myself together, got up, and started walking in the rain. I loved the Autumn rainfall when the cold wind blows and whispers through the valley. There were piles of leaves all over the ground. It was so quiet I started dragging my feet through the piles of leaves. I walked a good couple of hours so no one could see me crying or hear my despair.

I kept telling myself to remain patient and not let anyone get to me. I could feel Antonio trying to steal kisses from me. My hands were so cold. I was holding the friendship ring tightly in my palm and when I opened my hand the imprint of the ring could be seen. I could never tell anyone about my ring because if they found out that I had met Antonio secretly I would have been severely punished. I was freezing under the umbrella and there was absolute silence in the forest. The snow was melting and I noticed the beautiful purple, white, and yellow violets through the cracks in the snow. I could only hear the raindrops and I made a wish. I wished Antonio and I would grow old together. The rain washed away my tears.

After two months there was still no word from Antonio and I started feeling let down and wondered if he would ever contact me. I stopped caring about anything anymore. I hoped that no one would blast me for not feeding the ducks or the chickens. One day as I was walking towards my house, pure white snow started to fall. I said to myself, "We will be together and everything will be as it was meant to be. I stopped to catch my breath and to watch the magic of the first pure white snow. I started crying like a little girl and the snow froze my tears just like that day with my Nonna when my tears had felt like ice on my cheeks. Sitting there hopelessly just like a child I couldn't say anything.

I kept my loneliness a secret from everyone as I didn't want my siblings to mock me. I finally returned home and when I walked into the house there was my beautiful Nonna spinning yarn and chestnuts roasting on the fire. The crackling of the fire and the purring of the cat made the atmosphere even more homely and welcoming. I sat on the window sill and watched as the snow kept falling. My Nonna asked me why I was wet. She began roasting orzo in the frying pan. Orzo is a substitute for coffee as back then we couldn't afford such a luxury. Nonna tapped me on the shoulder and said, "There, there, it's almost Christmas. I am spinning the yarn so you can dress the Christmas tree. I started laughing and crying at the same time. She looked at me and said, "It is a beautiful fact that you and I are together. We can make some precious holiday memories." I didn't want to hear that as it seemed my life was small. I wanted to break the barriers of reason and fly to where Antonio was. I was tired of the constant reminder from my siblings that Antonio was not coming. Nonna recognised the hurt and loneliness behind my sad smile. Christmas came and went with no news of Antonio.

Chapter Six

I finally heard from the love of my life. Antonio explained that when he returned to Australia, he had started the process of getting all the papers sorted so I could come to Australia to be his wife. He also said that as my parents and two of my siblings could not afford to travel, he decided not only to pay for my family to come to Australia but also to sponsor us so we could all live in this great country. His parents showed immense generosity by letting us live in one of their houses until my father could afford to buy his own.

So, the wedding plans were set in motion but first, an engagement party had to be organised. I bought a pretty floor-length purple dress embroidered with flowers which cost me three weeks' wages. I was employed as an assistant to a chef in a restaurant so I picked up extra shifts whenever I could, to pay for my dress as my parents couldn't help me financially. I picked up the dress on the day of the engagement.

After three months in Australia, we held the engagement at Mrs McCain's grand house. She had a most stunning room at the back of her home. It even had a baby grand piano. As I walked into the room that evening I felt like a princess, but the tradition was that I couldn't see the engagement ring until it was placed on my finger by my fiancé. It was a beautiful ring and I was taken aback by the large solitaire. I had hoped for a modest ring like my friend had received from her fiancé. I was only 16 at the time and didn't appreciate how lucky I was to receive such an expensive ring.

Our engagement party was very intimate with only the immediate family and a few close friends. My father worked two jobs to pay for the engagement party. I was having a good time playing with the children instead of engaging with the older guests. My future mother-in-law didn't approve of this behaviour and swiftly pulled me aside. The rest of the night went well.

A couple of months after the engagement my future mother-in-law came to pay my mother and me a visit. She told us that the wedding had to be the best that money could buy. She had a reputation to uphold as her family's livelihood was hosting functions and also that she only had one son. She also told my mother that no expense should be spared on the wedding dress. My mother became very stressed as my family could not afford to spend so much money. When my future mother-in-law left, my mother disappeared into her bedroom and I could hear her crying. I went to see why she was crying and she explained that they couldn't afford an expensive wedding dress or the kind of wedding that they were expected to host. I was upset for my parents so I spoke to Antonio about it and explained what had occurred and how upset my mother was. He told me not to worry and that he would take care of everything. As good as my mother-in-law was she was also very controlling. She ordered my wedding dress and had it sent out from Italy. She organised the whole wedding. Though I couldn't choose what I wanted, luckily her taste was impeccable.

Our special day arrived. It was the 8th of February. We had an extravagant wedding with 700 guests. There was so much activity happening in the house. Two wedding planners arrived to decorate the house. The hallway had a high ceiling with gorgeous French doors. The planners filled the hallway with pink and white balloons and lots of pink and white roses were placed around the house. The doorbell kept ringing continuously. Antonio had organised a delivery of 40 champagne glasses, four bottles of Moet Champagne, and a few trays of assorted chocolates. My parents were overwhelmed by his generosity. The truth was that my mother-in-law wanted everything to be perfect when the whole thing was being filmed and while taking photographs.

My father kept pacing the floor while my mum was running around like a headless chook. She was preparing platters of food for family members and close friends who would be arriving shortly. It is an Italian custom that the close family attends the bride's house before the church ceremony to have a drink and nibbles to congratulate the family. She dressed the table with a beautiful white embroidered linen tablecloth which she had brought over from Italy. Mum did a wonderful job and she was pleased with the outcome.

In the meantime, I was very nervous as well as excited. At 8 am there was a knock at my door. My dress as well as a make-up artist/hairdresser had arrived. The hairdresser attempted an upstyle with my hair, but it was a nightmare as my hair was so long and the flowers just wouldn't stay in. She persisted and finally, it held. My mother-in-law paid for her services for the whole day and night to make sure I looked impeccable throughout the ceremony. My make-up was simplistic and my nails were freshly painted. I put on my beautiful princess-style wedding dress. It was made of French lace and satin and had gorgeous puffy sleeves. I also had a 5-metre-long veil which was perfect. I was ready to go to the church to marry the love of my life.

Finally, I was ready and I saw my papa waiting for me in the passage. He was the first person to see me in my wedding dress. He hugged me with tears in his eyes, his voice trembling with emotion as he looked at me and said, "Smile at everyone and don't get too emotional. The bells of the church are ringing with joy for both of you. It seems like yesterday when I was holding you and rocking you in my arms while singing La Nina Nana and today you are my beautiful precious princess. You look like the most beautiful bride in the world, an Angel from heaven." As we stepped outside through the back door, the wedding planners released six white rabbits with pink bows around their necks. This was all for show and had been organised by my mother-in-law. I am not sure why she did this but who am I to question her?

Two black Cadillacs arrived to collect my bridal party and me. We were half an hour late to the church and Antonio was worried, but everything had to be perfect and so it was. As I approached the church in the wedding car, I could see people standing outside and I became very nervous and had butterflies in my

stomach. Coming from a small town in Italy I had never seen so many people attend a wedding ceremony before. My father was walking me down the aisle and I will never forget how handsome and proud he looked. Then I saw Antonio and he had such a big smile on his face that my heart melted. The orchestra began to play and the vocalist sang Ave Maria as I walked on my father's arm just as I had dreamed since I was a little girl. As I got closer to the front of the church, I noticed my future husband had tears in his eyes. My father looked at me with his beautiful big blue eyes and he also shed a tear. I had never seen my father cry before. As I stood by Antonio's side he told me that I looked as beautiful as a goddess.

Once we exchanged our wedding vows, we walked back down the aisle as husband and wife. We were showered with fresh pink rose petals, confetti rice, and pink, white and blue sugared almonds. Our guests came up and congratulated us by kissing and hugging us. Once this was over, we all went to get out photos taken at the Botanical Gardens in the city. It was a beautiful warm day (29 degrees). The day seemed to be going by so quickly that it felt like a dream.

The wedding reception was everything I had ever dreamed of and more. My favourite colour was pink and when I walked into the reception centre there were masses of pink roses and white orchids everywhere, it was spectacular. From start to finish the wedding reception was everything my mother-in-law said it would be. Our guests enjoyed an evening filled with food, music, and a floor show. Antonio never left my side the whole evening. We did all the traditional elements of a wedding, cutting the seven-tier wedding cake, throwing the garter, and throwing the wedding bouquet.

Antonio and I opened the dance floor with a Roberta Flack song "Tonight I celebrate my love for you". He was a magnificent dancer. Our guests carried out the traditional wrapping of the bride and groom with streamers. The streamers are attached to the hands of the couple and when they start dancing the guests hold the streamers so that the couple gets wrapped up. This is a symbol of good wishes from the guests. Once our wedding song was over we freed ourselves from the streamers and then suddenly we heard the beating of drums. Two men were walking towards the dance floor while beating the drums. They put on an incredible performance. Once their performance ended, my father came up to me on the dance floor and the band started playing La Tarantella, a dance performed by the guests to wish good luck to the newly married couple. The guests hold hands and rotate clockwise as the music speeds up and then they reverse the direction. All the guests followed my dad's lead, everyone had a great time.

Antonio delivered his speech which included a beautiful poem:

> "You will always be my shining star and if I shall die before you, I will search heaven and earth to find you,
>
> And if I can't find you there, I will carve your name
>
> In every star, so everyone on earth will know,
>
> how much I love you, Bella."

He also gifted me a huge bunch of red roses with rolls of money tucked between the buds. I was confused as to why he felt it necessary to gift me money since the roses were as it is a beautiful and loving gesture on their own.

Antonio and I left the reception approximately at midnight. We walked through the arch which our guests made by holding their hands over their heads and clasping the other person's hands opposite them. We bid them all farewell and someone drove us to an expensive 5-Star Hotel in the city. The groom carried me over the threshold and I was in absolute awe as I had never seen a room so lavish and beautiful as this one was. I felt overwhelmed and nervous at the same time.

Antonio poured us champagne and I started relaxing a little. We started getting tipsy and Antonio grabbed me and kissed me passionately. He was eager for me to take off my wedding dress. I asked him to undo the little pearl buttons but he was very impatient and ripped my dress. I began to cry as I was upset by this. I was worried about what I would tell my mother-in-law when she would see the ripped dress. I became very distressed and Antonio just held me in his arms so our marriage wasn't consummated that evening.

The next day the celebrations continued. It is an Italian tradition that the day after the wedding a family gathering is hosted at the groom's parents' home. But on this day Antonio took me to a different address and not to his parent's home. I had never been to this place before. When we walked around to the back of the house all our family yelled out "surprise". I was shocked as I wasn't sure what was happening.

All in the Name of Love

My mother-in-law approached us and handed us a key and said, "this house is your wedding gift from me." We were speechless. Such a generous gesture! It was a beautiful 2-storey house fully furnished with the most beautiful furniture. The pillars at the front were painted pink, my favourite colour.

We had a barbeque lunch and since it was a warm day I wore my black leather shorts, a red tube top, and green high platform shoes. My cousins were being silly and grabbed the stool I was sitting on and threw me and the stool into the pool. They didn't know I couldn't swim but Antonio knew and he became very distressed and jumped in to pull me out of the water. My mother-in-law ushered me inside and found me something to wear. It was a floral long dress to my ankles which wasn't something I was used to wearing. I asked my mum, "Do I look alright?" and she responded yes you do and laughed under her breath when she walked away as I usually wore miniskirts and shorts. I then asked my sister if I looked okay and she responded, "Hmm" she said, "Now you look just like her", referring to my mother-in-law and she also laughed.

During lunch, my mother-in-law pulled me aside and asked me about the previous night. She asked me if I was sore and I didn't understand what she meant by this comment. I asked my mother what my mother-in-law was implying. My mother blushed and said, "Sweetheart what she wanted to know was if you were sore after having sex." I told my mother what had happened the previous evening and that we ultimately didn't have sex. I felt so embarrassed since I was still a virgin and didn't know what to expect.

In the end, everyone had a good day and finally, the guests started leaving.

We went inside the house with our parents as it was time to open the gifts and the wedding cards. We received some beautiful crystal and China gifts which I still have to this day. We were also gifted a considerable amount of money.

Then it was time for our parents to leave and finally, we were left alone. Antonio ran a bubble bath, and lit some candles in the bathroom and bedroom; there were rose petals on the bed placed in the shape of a love heart with sugared almonds and money strewn over the bed. It was another Italian tradition that the night before the wedding the mother of the bride and the mother of the groom make up the matrimonial bed with white linen sheets. This represents purity. Antonio opened a bottle of champagne for us. We both sat in the bath and reminisced about the wedding and that day. We were making small talk until my nerves faded away. That night we consummated our marriage. He was very caring and gentle and made me feel at ease and special.

The next morning dot at 8 am there was a knock on our front door. Antonio and I were still in bed. It surprised us and Antonio ran to the door to see who it was. It was his mother. He quickly called out to me to let me know that she was there and asked me to come into the kitchen. I quickly put on my robe and ran downstairs. We started chatting about how beautiful the wedding had been and the previous day's BBQ. I made a few croissants and coffee. My mother-in-law disappeared and I thought she was going to the bathroom. But I saw her coming down the stairs with our bed sheets in her arms and then she left hastily. I was confused by this so I called my mother and told her what had happened. My mother said that she was checking the sheets to see if there was any blood because then she would know whether you were a virgin. My mother said, "Bella, you have nothing to hide. You have done nothing wrong." But unfortunately, Antonio's mother was so old-fashioned that if she didn't see any blood she would have disowned my family and me. It never came to this.

Chapter Seven

A week later we went overseas for our honeymoon. We first went to Italy and based ourselves at my Nonna's house for two weeks. It was winter and very cold. I could touch the snow-covered trees from my balcony. They had icicles hanging from them.

One day Antonio went with my cousins to hunt for a wild pig. I remained at home with Nonna. She was a great storyteller. She made us a hot drink and we settled in so she could start her story. The story was about a midwife who lived in the woods by herself. When this woman was about 14 years of age she lived with her father in a cottage in the woods far away from the village as her mother had passed away when she was a small child. One day she was walking home alone from school when she was raped. Back in the day, no man wanted to marry her because she had been assaulted.

This woman became a midwife and delivered children as she didn't have any of her own. In due course of time, her father passed away and she continued staying alone in the cottage. One day at about 5 pm she was sitting at home in front of the crackling fire when someone knocked on her door. This wasn't unusual as people were always fetching her to deliver babies as she was the only midwife for miles around and people trusted her. It was very windy and she could hardly keep the door open. Outside a monk-like man was standing dressed in a brown robe like a monk. He had a hessian bag on his head to protect him from the rain and he held a large wooden stick with a carved serpent on the top.

He asked the woman if he could spend the night in her house as he had to travel far and the weather was bad. The woman refused saying, "No, I am a respected midwife and what will people say?" She asked him to leave and just as he turned away the heavens opened and it started raining very heavily with thunder. She felt sorry for him so she called him and told him that he could stay. She gave him a cushion and said he could sleep in front of the fire. She warned him that if he made one move away from the fireplace she would have to ask him to leave. She also said that she might be called out during the night to deliver babies. And it just so happened, she was called several times that night. And every time she returned the man knew the sex of the baby and their names and made predictions about what would happen to the babies in the future. She didn't think much of it at that time as she was very tired from being up most of the night.

In the early hours of the morning, as the weather cleared, she asked the man to leave. But before he left she wanted to know how he knew the names, sex, and the future of the babies. He said the first child born during the night was Mario who at the age of 22 would fall off a horse and die. The second child born was Elisabetta who will get married and raise three children and live happily. The third child born that night was Vito who will travel the world and preach the word of the Lord. She looked curiously at him and asked, "Who are you? Are you a magician?" He replied, "I am Destiny. Once a child is born I hand out their destiny which cannot be changed. She then asked him to reverse Mario's destiny and he said that once a destiny is written it cannot be reversed or changed.

Saying this, he tapped his stick three times on the floor and then he vanished into thin air. The woman was shocked to witness this. She went to pick up the cushion and under it, she found three rose petals with a little note saying, "God has heard your prayer, you will be rewarded for the work you do in safely delivering children into the world". This story unsettled me as I found it quite disturbing and I couldn't even go to the bathroom on my own that night as the bathroom was outside in the dark. Antonio had to accompany me. We stayed at Nonna's for another week and then we moved on to Antonio's parents' hometown.

His extended family were beautiful people, very warm and hospitable. They had a tobacco farm and were very proud and generous people. They took us sightseeing and we went to Napoli, Pompeii, Sorrento, Positano, and Amalfi to name a few destinations. Before we knew it, we were off to Paris where we spent a whole week. We then travelled back to Nonna's house to collect our stuff as it was time to head back home to Australia. I had enough time to go for a walk. I didn't go too far and sat on top of a hill watching the sunset. I started crying because I was going to miss my Nonna terribly. Saying goodbye to her would be the hardest thing I had ever done in my life as I loved my Nonna more than my mother. We were very close. I knew in my heart of hearts that this would be the last time I would be with her. I cried a river of tears and felt an unbearable ache in my heart. I was starting to feel numb with sadness.

I pulled myself together and went back to say my goodbyes to Nonna. She hugged me so hard that I could hardly breathe and she whispered in my ear, "I have no precious gifts to give you, but I have four words - Darling, I love you". That was the last time I physically hugged my amazing Nonna Antonietta.

I think the only reason people hold on so tightly to memories for so long is because memories are the only things that don't change even when people do.

Chapter Eight

Antonio and I resumed our married lives when we returned home. We went back to work and life became normal. Two months later I had a very special announcement to make. I was two months pregnant with my first baby boy. My husband invited the whole family and close friends and told them the good news. Antonio handed out cigars. Everyone was excited and congratulated us. We both were really happy. A week later, I remember it was a Wednesday, I started feeling nauseous. So, I rang my mother-in-law to let her know I would not be coming to work. She was very understanding and said to ring her if I needed anything.

That evening it was around 7 o'clock and my husband was still not home from work. There was a knock at the door. It was my mother-in-law and as soon as she saw me she said that I looked awful. And I thought what did she expect when I had been throwing up all day? She had very high expectations when it came to my appearance. She said that if I was tired I should learn to rest. I couldn't help myself and answered her sternly, "How am I going to rest if you expect me to work seven days a week?" My mother-in-law could see I wasn't myself so she made me a cup of camomile tea to settle my stomach. I thought it was a lovely gesture. Then she started telling me that she was going to choose the baby's name as it was her first grandson. I replied in a resigned tone, "I guess I have no say?"

I had very high blood pressure, so I was admitted to the hospital for seven days. Antonio came to visit me every night after work. The nurses always commented on how attentive and handsome he was.

At the end of my pregnancy, I gave birth to a healthy baby boy weighing 8 pounds and he was 22 inches long. He was really beautiful. He had fair hair. My mother-in-law named him David. As usual, she always got her way. My room was filled with flowers from well-wishers. My husband was so happy that he handed out cigars and celebrated all evening with his friends, smoking cigars and drinking cognac.

Nine months later I became pregnant again with my second son, Massimo. He was a pleasant baby. He stole my heart. When I saw him for the first time I started crying as I felt truly blessed.

Before Massimo was born I had a message for my eldest.

David was such a good baby but deep down I longed for a baby girl. Before his birth, I had picked out everything in pink along with a little brown bear and a white Peter Rabbit. Nevertheless, I loved him with all my heart.

When it was time to baptize David, as usual, my mother-in-law arranged everything. She arrived at our house in the morning. She was wearing a beautiful show-stopping long blue dress. I prepared coffee, liquor, and nibbles for the guests. The godparents dressed David in a beautiful traditional white lace christening gown with an accompanying lace hat. He looked like an angel. My handsome husband wore a blue wool suit and eventually even I changed into a long backless red satin dress with red gloves.

The baptism was held at the same church where we had been married and it was breathtaking. There were a whole lot of beautiful white flowers and candles. When the priest poured the Holy water onto David's head he started screaming. I grabbed him from his godmother's arms and placed my little finger into his mouth so he would settle. My mother-in-law gave me the biggest dagger. If looks could kill, I would have been one dead duck. After the ceremony, we proceeded to take photos inside and outside the church.

The party was held at an Argentinian restaurant in the city. We only had family and close friends. When we arrived my mother-in-law quickly took David out of my arms as if he was a trophy. I let her do so as this gave me an opportunity to mingle with the guests and have a couple of drinks. I was getting tipsy and started giggling like a schoolgirl. My mother-in-law told my sister that she was not impressed with me and that I was making a fool of myself. I wasn't taking any notice of her and in my head, I could hear my Nonna's voice loud and clear, "Remember to look up to the stars and not down at your feet, try to make sense of what you hear and see and what makes the universe exist. Be patient and curious at the same time. However difficult life may seem there is always something you can do to succeed. It matters that you don't give up". So, I tried really hard to understand my mother-in-law. Believe

All in the Name of Love

me, it wasn't easy but I tried to accept her for who she was.

At eighteen years of age, I was pregnant with my second child. To my dearest David, you are the air that I breathe and you are the one who first made me a mother. You were the one that first opened my heart in ways I never knew possible. You are my biggest weakness yet you give me the greatest strength. Over the last few months, I have watched you grow which has filled me with so much pride and joy. Knowing that in a few months, you will be a big brother has hit me in ways I didn't think were possible. It has been emotional to think that you are no longer going to be my only baby. You are strong, you are loving, you are resilient and you will teach your baby brother things I never can. I am going to watch you feel things that I can't protect you from.

David, it will no longer be just the two of us against the world. To say that out loud doesn't make me feel scared, sad, or happy, it just fills me with love. Thank you for teaching me how to be a mum. Together we have learned the way. I can't wait to tackle our next adventure of being a mother for me and a brother for you. I want you to know that you will forever be my firstborn and that will never change no matter how old you are or who else enters your life. David, I love you with all that I am. I pray that you know how grateful I am that you chose me to be your mum. I always want you to know that you will never be alone. We are just navigating together through this new chapter of life and I will always be by your side, loving and protecting you. I cannot wait to watch you grow up.

I worked alongside my mother-in-law in her catering business until the last week of my second pregnancy. Once again, she picked a name for my son. I was a lot older and said to her, "I will pick the name myself this time". Needless to say, she wasn't impressed and she didn't keep her anger to herself as she made sure I knew how angry she was. When Massimo was born, out of spite for me she didn't even buy him a gift. Massimo looked just like me and my husband and I was truly blessed to have two beautiful boys.

Two weeks after I came home from the hospital after giving birth to Massimo, I turned 19. I remember it very well. It was a cold and wet winter day. The Sun would come out now and then while I was sitting in front of a large open fireplace. Antonio had replicated the fireplace we had seen in a tiny town in Italy called San Jamyne. It was made of stone and was beautiful. My newborn was sleeping like an angel in his crib and my eldest was sleeping in my arms. I was in awe of how beautiful my two boys were. I wanted them to wake up but in all honesty, I couldn't disturb them. I sat there feeling truly blessed.

My children were the world to me and I loved my sons more than anything in this world as they were my masterpieces. From the day we looked into each other's eyes I believed in miracles. I believed that they were both God's gifts to me. Both have given me some of the most beautiful and precious moments. As a mother, every day I teach them strength and passion and to love each other and to carry that through their entire life and one day when I am old and grey and they no longer need me as they go into this crazy world that we live in, they would look back and say, "She wasn't perfect, but she was our mum".

As long as I am breathing you will always be the love of my life and I will always teach you that respect is one of the greatest expressions of love. Always remember my sweet boys that I have been honest, loyal, and true. I appreciate the simple things in life and I will not change or harden to this world. It is this sensitivity, perception, sincerity, affection and gentle grace that makes me who I am. That day a silent wind opened the window for the sunlight to come in. As you grow up you must understand that the wind brings the Sun and light of life and there will be times when you won't understand some things or there might be circumstances that upset you. But, always remember that you will have a loyal companion in me. I will always be around until I take my last breath. That's all I have to offer you.

Even after three years of marriage, I was still very attracted to my husband as he was smoking hot, and the sex was magical. I used to love watching him as he took a shower, it left me breathless. I adored washing his hair in the shower.

The boys were growing up fast and I was busy tending to them and their needs. Antonio was always working to provide for our little family, and he started feeling like he was being neglected. That is when I started seeing another side of him.

Antonio's business was thriving. He purchased a beautiful, limited edition red Alfa Romeo sports car for himself. He took all of us to the beach for a drive and Massimo wanted to walk on the sand, but Antonio wouldn't allow it as he didn't want sand in his new car. I saw a side of Antonio that I didn't like. He cared more about the car than the kids. This upset Massimo and he started crying loudly. Antonio couldn't care less as he just wanted to show his authority to the boys at this young age. On another occasion, we were on our way to dinner as a family and one of the boys let off some gas. He pulled over and threw him out of the car. The child would have been just 10 years of age. At first, I thought Antonio was joking and just wanted to assert his authority, but he was very serious so I also got out of the car and started walking home with my son. Antonio never turned around to pick us up. It was a long walk home; we didn't have mobile phones back then.

When I was turning 21 my husband organised a surprise for me. He hired a private jet and as we were walking towards the plane suddenly the door opened, and pink helium balloons poured out. We flew out to Hamilton Island. When we arrived at the luxury hotel we checked in and proceeded to our hotel room. Antonio picked me up and threw me onto the bed. He said, "Can you believe that even after five years you still have this effect on me". He took my hand and placed it on his erection. I gasped and slightly tightened my hand around his girth and he said he wanted to feel my warmth. He was glancing into my eyes as he was undressing me and then we both fell naked onto the bed. Once again, he said he wanted to be inside me to feel my warmth and I said while glaring at him, "Take me now, fuck me".

His mouth dropped and I asked him, "What are you going to do with me?" He gently caressed my clitoris with his erect penis. I then pushed him onto his back, he laughed and I gazed down at him feeling glorious. He responded by saying, "I am going to explode" as I was rubbing his erect penis. Feeling the hair in his oh-so-happy trail he closed his eyes and flexed his hips. "You will have to learn to keep still" I scolded, and tugged on his long hair. His breathing was getting shallower and he grinned at me, "Yes, Miss Bella" he murmured, eyes burning bright in the vehement sensation pulsing through me. Our eyes locked and almost for a split second, I was in absolute ecstasy. I was in charge; he was all mine and I was his. After our sensual encounter, Antonio said, "I didn't know you had that in you". I responded with a mischievous smile, "That was my gift to you".

That evening we went out for a beautiful dinner and had drinks at the bar. My husband really knew how to spoil me. There was a pianist playing jazz music in the background. We had an amazing night together. Around 1 am we went back to our hotel room. An absolutely beautiful vision was in front of me. Antonio had arranged for candles and pink rose petals to be placed around our room. He then blindfolded me and I thought to myself, "Mmm, what are you up to?" He then grabbed my hand and placed a gorgeous white gold and diamond bracelet on my wrist. I was speechless. Antonio dropped the thin straps of my dress off my shoulders and my silk Pisello dress fell to the floor. I stood there topless and in my suspenders, the belt holding up my silk stockings and a G-string. He couldn't get enough of me that night. It was so intense and sensual. It was one of the best nights we had ever had.

We spent a whole week together, sightseeing and reconnecting on a sexual level. Antonio spoilt me rotten. I had a great time and it remains one of my favourite times spent with him. However, it was time to return home to reality. I was missing my boys and couldn't wait to see and hold them.

Chapter Nine

As a young mother, my life was very hard, juggling my work, kids, and home. Returning to work was very difficult for me but I did what I had to do.

One day when I was at work one of my friends dropped in for a hot meal. I stopped work to have a chat with her and my mother-in-law scolded me for doing so. She didn't have a very active role at the shop, she just stood back and watched the staff so when it was quiet she always picked on me. One day I had enough and I answered her back, "Trust, respect, and loyalty are earned and I would give you plenty of all. But the betrayal of any one of these is to lose all three. We all have our bad days and no one is perfect. So, if you have had a shit day, have a big glass of wine, call a friend and bitch about it, eat some chocolate, and then jump into bed and watch a movie. Tomorrow is a new day."

My mother-in-law was not at all happy with what I said. She didn't waste any time in ringing my husband to tell him what had happened to me. At home that night my husband told me that she had called him. I started giggling. I put the boys to bed and then grabbed a shower. Antonio came into the shower with me and started washing my back. I was taken by surprise as he was being rough and I asked him, "What's gotten into you? You are hurting me". He apologised and got out of the shower. I got into bed and he instantly flipped me over and produced a whip. He began whipping me. I screamed for him to stop as he was really hurting me. My eldest son came into our room and asked his dad, "What are you doing to my mummy?" His father responded, "Nothing, we are just playing a game, go back to bed".

When I mentioned the incident between myself and my mother-in-law to one of my siblings she quickly replied, "It's the old goat, she is miserable and she wants you to be miserable as well". I was determined that I wouldn't let my mother-in-law get to me. Self-control is strength, calmness is a mystery. I needed to get to a point where her mood wouldn't affect me. I didn't want to let her actions control the direction of my life. I didn't want to allow her emotions to overpower my intelligence. I never wanted to seek a perfect life, I just wanted to be happy and be surrounded by good friends who loved me for who I was. I was disappointed but not surprised and it has been one of my life lessons. I don't want to be around drama, conflict, or stress. I wanted a cosy home, enjoy good food and wine and be around happy people like when I was a young girl. Even though our family didn't have much, but we always looked out for each other and had each other's back. We all sat together and laughed together. All my in-laws family ever talked about was business.

I learned a long time ago that you can't beg someone to love you. I am too good to change someone who does not know my worth and I am too wild to keep waiting

All in the Name of Love

for someone who doesn't acknowledge my value. I want and deserve to be loved unconditionally; I shouldn't have to fight for it. I don't have the time and I won't prove to someone that I am worth it. My self-worth is more than that. At that time I felt as if I was always in a battle with my mother-in-law and I was the loser as she was so much stronger than me. However, it doesn't matter how educated, talented, or wealthy you believe you are as it doesn't mean a thing if you don't treat people with integrity and dignity. Integrity is everything. Despite our differences, I do believe that deep down she loved me in her own way, but she never showed it to me and she just bought material things for me. That was her way of showing me that she cared.

I was raised to treat others like I would like to be treated. I would give my seat up for another if they needed it and would always be available to lend a helping hand to others. I was never one to watch from the sidelines. In return, I expected to be treated in the same manner. I also taught my children to be proud of who they were. They are a reflection of me. I was certain of one thing that even though my family wasn't perfect but we were very proud and we always stuck together. Nonna was important and she will always live in my thoughts. Back then I wanted to stay near her and watch over her just as she did when I was a young girl. But Nonna refused to leave her home and one day my auntie found her dead in her bed.

Nonna passed away with the knowledge that we all lived in a perfect world, and I always remember her amazing manners. Rest Nonna until we meet again. Her favourite word was 'amore' which means love in Italian and thank you was always on her lips. Sometimes when I lay on my bed deep in my thoughts, my vision becomes so clear that I start conversing with her. I can hear her soft voice singing me a lullaby. It didn't matter to her that I was a grown woman. Nonna would sing this one lullaby, "Sleep baby, sleep baby this music that is playing will put you to sleep, sleep my angel sleep". I used to sing the very same lullaby to my two boys. I always felt her presence around me. I felt she was always watching over me and it gave me a sense of peace and protection.

As my boys were growing up, I started telling them about my Nonna. Two days before Christmas we were putting up the Christmas tree and I explained to them that when I was growing up we didn't have beautiful decorations or a tall tree that almost reached the ceiling. I told them that we decorated our tree with the white wool from our sheep and we tied the wool into bows. Once we finished putting up the tree my boys and I sat under it holding hands remembering all those people who had left us. Nonna, we remember you in the morning until we look up at the stars in the evening. You will always be with us. Sometimes in life, a heartbreak jolts you awake and reminds you that you are worth more than what you were settling for.

Chapter Ten

At the age of 33, I decided to leave my husband as I was drowning in my sorrow, feelings, and emotions. At the same time, I was petrified of being on my own with my children. I was determined to leave as I had had enough. I was scared when I confronted Antonio but he convinced me to stay and before I knew it things were back to square one.

I was settling for very little as Antonio was working long hours and I was the one keeping everything together for our family. At the young age of 22, I had a full-time job, I was looking after my two children and maintaining and running a house. I was mentally and physically exhausted. I would fall asleep as soon as I finished my chores in the evening. Every time I told Antonio that I was tired his response was, "What have you done all day?" I started resenting him and loving him less. I put up with his behaviour and words for a long time. Finally, it got to a point where I couldn't take it anymore. I learned that things don't always turn out the way you plan. I have learnt that things go wrong and don't get fixed or put back together the way they were if you don't do anything. I have learnt that some broken things stay broken and that I am a strong person and I can get through the bad times and keep looking for a better way as long as I love myself.

Before I decided to leave Antonio I noticed that every time we went to an event, he would leave me sitting on my own while he did his rounds. If I asked him for a dance, he would accept only to show people that we were the happiest couple. One night we had gone to a function where he was being awarded the Italian Man of the Year. That evening I had a sore foot so I kept sitting the whole time. He danced the night away with a woman called Rosa. While dancing with my husband this woman kept glancing on and off at me. When they finished dancing, Antonio went to talk to someone and Rosa approached me. She had the nerve to ask me, "How did you manage to get a man as handsome as Antonio?" I was so angry that I responded, "It was the power of my pussy that he couldn't resist". She laughed and Antonio quickly came to see what we were talking about. I told him what Rosa had said and he was not happy. He looked at her and said, "How dare you speak to my wife like that". She apologised and blamed her behaviour on having had too many drinks. Finally, it was time to leave. When we got home Antonio was feeling amorous but I was feeling tired.

The next morning I got up to make coffee but Antonio was cold toward me. My husband always held a grudge if he didn't get his way. I was sick of this behaviour of his. When I first met him, I was so in love with him but now it was like a heavy pain in my heart. I felt that my life wasn't mine anymore. I didn't say anything to him as a hundred thoughts, problems and issues were running through my mind. I wasn't happy with the situation, in my own head. I thought, "This isn't a healthy relationship. I can't continue this relationship as it feels impossible, but then I kept remembering our wedding vows and the guilt would creep in. I kept telling myself, "Our love is deeper than the sea, stronger than a hurricane, timid like a breeze, and a bond between two hearts, a symphony of feelings even when we are apart. But I was in denial and my confidence was badly bruised. I felt as though he was manipulating and controlling me.

One evening Antonio returned home from work. He mentioned in passing that he was going to Italy on business the following week. He went off to Italy for three months. Every time I spoke to him on the phone asking when he would be returning home he kept saying, "I haven't settled the business yet". I became suspicious and asked my mother-in-law to look after the children so I could fly to Italy. Antonio didn't know. I wanted to surprise him. When I arrived in Italy I stayed for a week with my Nonna. Then I rang him to pick me up in Naples.

I landed in Rome and organised for my cousin to pick me up from the airport. I spent a week on my own in Rome. I caught a train to my hometown. I was overwhelmed by the scenery as it was almost desolate. It brought back so many childhood memories. I was walking towards the three fountains and started taking photographs. I dangled my feet into the fountain soaking them in the water. I heard a loud echo through the valley. I put on my shoes and went to investigate. I remembered the road so clearly. A very old man was sitting on a bench on the road. He had his back to me, so

I yelled out "Hello". He asked me my name and I told him who my parents were, but he couldn't recall my dad. I then proceeded to tell him my Nonna's name and he immediately knew who she was. He told me he had gone to school with Antonietta and that he loved her very much, but her father had promised her to someone else and she was married at the age of 14. I said Nonna had never told me about him. He said he couldn't bear to see her getting married as she was so beautiful and everyone in this small town loved her.

So, on the morning of her wedding, before the bells of the church rang, he went off to Milano to pursue his studies. Eventually, he became a police officer. When his sister would visit him he always enquired about Antonietta's well-being. He told his sister that he was still in love with her. His sister told him how she was mistreated by her husband and on one occasion he had kicked her so hard that he had broken her shoulder. Antonietta was petrified of her husband. He told his sister to ask her to come to him and to tell her husband word for word what exactly he was saying. "I will kill him". His sister told her parents and that night they shipped my Nonna's husband, my grandfather, off to America and he never returned.

I didn't know any of this and I asked him to tell me a little more about Nonna and her youth. His eyes lit up like a candle. He never married as she was his only true love. He invited me to his house for a coffee and we spent half the night talking about Nonna. I got up in the morning and went outside to drink my coffee. The view was so picturesque that it seemed as if I was looking at a postcard. I picked a fig off a tree and devoured it. It was delicious. Mario had this big smile on his face and said to me, "I named that fig tree Julia", after your Nonna's best friend who was almost as beautiful as your Nonna and had a voice like an angel. Julia worked so hard on the land but her husband was so jealous of her singing that he demanded she not sing anymore. One afternoon while working the land Julia's co-workers begged her to sing but she hesitated because she was afraid of her husband. After being forced further by her co-workers she started singing. Her beautiful voice echoed through the whole valley.

That afternoon when she returned home her husband was waiting for her. Julia was picking a fig off the tree and her husband started yelling at her, "I told you not to sing". He was holding an axe in his hand and he went crazy and started hitting her with it. Julia didn't survive the attack.

Mario proceeded to tell me how he bought the house as he knew that my Nonna would come to pick the figs and feel close to Julia. I recalled this as a child. My Nonna was an only child and everyone adored and loved her. She was left to raise three kids on her own. I asked him why he didn't go after her when she was left alone. He replied, "Beautiful Bella, I couldn't as I would have brought shame to her family and I didn't want that for her." I thanked Mario for his hospitality and for reminiscing with me. That afternoon I boarded a train from Rome to Naples.

My husband was waiting for me at the train station. I was very happy to see him but he was very cold towards me. His family had prepared a delicious meal of lasagne, grilled fish, and salad. It was nice catching up with everyone. It was 11 o'clock and I was feeling tired so I excused myself and went to bed. My husband came to bed at 1 am and I desperately wanted him to make love to me. So, I instigated sex. We made love but my husband was a changed man. From that time on he didn't show any interest in me except when he wanted to show me off. I became his punching bag. He would also abuse me verbally. His words were sharp and cut me like a knife. Whenever we went somewhere and I looked at another man he would cuss me and accuse me of wanting to fuck them. My life was becoming a living hell. He was no longer the man I had fallen in love with. I started disliking him more and more. It came to a point where I couldn't even stand to hear the sound of his voice. I didn't know how to tell him that our marriage was over and that I had no feelings or love for him anymore.

I started composing a list of all the things that I wanted to say to him. I knew that if I didn't have it written down my hands would start shaking and my heart would beat so hard and fast that I wouldn't be able to hear my thoughts. One evening when Antonio returned home, I sat him down and as I stared at him I finally found the words to say, "I wish you could read my mind so you could see the sadness that lives inside me. I wish you could feel my grief. I have nothing else to give you. You used to be the air that I breathed and now we can't stand each other. I gave up everything for you but you tossed me aside like trash, forever talking me down." He responded, "Who would have you with two kids". I quickly went to let his mother know that we were splitting up and what Antonio had said. She responded with, "You aren't going to find anyone better than him. Who is going to have a woman with two kids?" I turned towards her and said, "Time will tell" and went my own way.

I applied for a job in a restaurant, and I became the head chef. I was rewarded for my work and was very proud of my achievement. I worked there for quite a few years. The kitchen was running like clockwork and I wasn't going to stay there forever. Ten years later it was time to say goodbye.

During that time I often thought of Antonio and how much he loved and cared for me. But it was time to move on. My marriage to Antonio was over. His family turned their back on me. They took Antonio's side and so did one of my sisters. She said awful things behind my back. I distanced myself from every one of them. I never lost faith in myself and I always had the support of my beautiful precious boys. They were my rock and we moved forward by starting a new life.

There are two things I am most proud of in my life and they are my beautiful children, David and Massimo. They both are compassionate and loving but both of them are different in their own way. Massimo grew up wanting to be just like his big brother, athletic and not to mention a little macho. He worked so hard for the day he could beat David at computer football or just simply have more information about every soccer player on every field. But David was different, and his dream was to become a model. He completed his modelling course and my husband and I encouraged him to chase his dreams, but his life was to take another road. My husband and I couldn't be prouder. We supported him every step of the way.

One of my life's greatest privileges was to be a part of his journey, a great privilege to be his mum. But my precious David was struggling with depression. I wanted to jump in and defend him, but Massimo held me back insisting that I should not travel down that road. The doctors kept telling me that I had to wait for him to own himself in time. I could make it easier only by standing on the side, loving him, and encouraging him to strive for his dreams. He can have the modelling career he always wanted and to also have a family of his own. But God had different plans for him, it wasn't David's choice. My child taught me many lessons and one of them is that they are the most precious gifts from Heaven.

My son, his generation, and the generations to follow will one day understand the illness he bears. I hope that one day they will find a cure for mental health and he would no longer feel ashamed that he was not able to achieve his dreams. It is a very hard long road when you stand on your own. I have always been there to love and support him in every possible way. My mind remembers from the minute he was born, his first step his first words but my heart remembers the feeling. The mind can forget but the heart remembers everything. The mind remembers the first words he spoke, but the heart remembers the feeling. The mind forgets but the heart never does.

As for my younger son Massimo, the struggle of his older brother played a very big part in his life but as a family, we pulled through. It seems hard today but we know that tomorrow will be a better day. Massimo is now a silver-service chef. He is a brilliant chef and runs his own restaurant. But he is very ruthless, it is his way or the highway. There is no in-between but at the same time he possesses a heart of gold and only a few people can see that. He stepped in and became the big brother. I know that the love he has for his brother is very deep. Someday we will forget the hurt, the reason we cried, and who caused us the pain and we will finally realize that he was part of his journey.

My beautiful boys have been through a lot together. Trust is like glass, once it is shattered it can never be perfect again. But every day for us is a new beginning and one thing that I have taught my boys is to give but don't allow yourself to be used or abused. Love but don't allow your heart to be abused. Trust but don't be naïve. Listen but don't judge, don't lose your voice and accept yourself for who you are and what you believe in. It is not your responsibility or your problem to accept everyone. If someone treats you badly just leave him and move on.

I will never forget my mother-in-law raising her voice and telling me that I will never be happy with anyone else. Those words played on my mind for a very long time. But I needed to move away from Antonio and move forward in my life. I loved Antonio since the day we met and no one has ever loved me as much as he did. But I had to find the strength to let him go. I asked one of my dearest friends for guidance and she replied, "Walk away and never look back". I was falling apart as my heart was breaking. So, I shut that door and walked away, there was nothing left to say. I know that there will be many moments of regret, but I don't want to turn around and don't want him to see me crying. My mother-in-law's words were so heavy, they came down on me like thunder and my tears were so heavy as if I was crying hail but I tried never to show them to anyone.

Chapter Eleven

I was enjoying my new life as a single woman and met some wonderful people along the way. I was also never short of a handsome man by my side, but I had no intentions of getting into a serious relationship. I loved going out to the clubs as I loved to dance. It was at one of these clubs that I met a handsome man with a smoking hot body named James. He worked with security at a particular club that I frequented. He was a bodybuilder and also an engineer. He caught my eye the first time I went to this club. Actually, as I was about to enter the premises I tripped and he caught me. I noticed that he kept an eye on me all night and when I was leaving he made sure he said goodnight and asked if I would be coming back soon. I told him politely that "I'd see how it goes."

The following week I got a phone call from a friend of mine called Angela inviting me to her partner's home for a dinner party. I was hesitant to go but Angela wouldn't take no for an answer. I arrived on time as I don't like being late. I was wearing a beautiful silk backless dress. I had had a busy day at work and hadn't eaten anything so I was starving. The dinner could not begin as one of the guests had not arrived. My patience was running thin as half an hour, then an hour, then an hour and a half passed and no one showed up. I approached my friend telling her that this was ridiculous and that we should start eating. She replied that it was her partner's best friend so we cannot start without him. I was angry. Finally, after waiting for two hours he arrived.

Who was this man? We had waited for none other than the security guard I had met at the club. He was so happy to see me again that he sat beside me at the table and finally dinner was served. He was so charming that my anger subsided. He said all the right things. We chatted for quite a while and I told him that my shoulders were sore so he promptly massaged them for me. I could see Angela's face. She was jealous and asked have you two fucked? I was shocked and said, "What are you talking about? We barely know each other."

The following week Angela called again to let me know that a group of friends were going out for dinner and asked me to come along. I was surprised as James was there again. We had a great time and that night he asked for my number. I replied that I was an old-fashioned girl and didn't have a phone. Unfortunately, that lie came unstuck because as we were leaving the restaurant to go to the club downstairs we ran into a doctor I was working with and he asked for my number as he had lost it. I was very embarrassed and James was very pissed off. He accused me of lying to him.

In the club, he bought our friends a round of drinks but he did not buy one for me. I didn't want to show that I was upset and at that moment a song I loved called Maria started playing. I went up to James and grabbed his hand and dragged him to the dance floor. As we danced the chemistry between us was electric. He ran his hands up and down my body and it made me weak in the knees. As he pulled my body towards him, I could feel his erect penis against my leg. A rush of excitement overwhelmed me. He held me tightly and kissed me passionately with his hands still roaming over my body. The smell of his skin made me feel like I had died and gone to heaven. I wanted him so badly.

We left the club and went back to my home where we made passionate love all night long. He pulled my dress off my body and blindfolded me with his tie and tied my hands with his belt. I was excited but scared at the same time as I didn't know what would happen next. His tongue was like a snake in my mouth, his touch made me shiver, he picked me up and threw me onto my bed, and started licking the back of my elevated leg. He started sucking my toes and worked his way to my vagina. He was aggressive but gentle at the same time. Sweat trickled down his back, his arms strong while my body was crying out for more. I finally felt like a woman again. This was the beginning of our erotic love affair.

A year later I would turn 40 and wanted to plan a party but James said he had to travel interstate on business and would not be able to attend. It drove me crazy to think that he was choosing business over me. Seeing how upset I was, Angela said fuck him and that she would take me to Sydney for my birthday. When we arrived in Sydney a limo was waiting for us and we were whisked away for a pampering day of massage and then onto a hairdresser. We spent the afternoon sipping Moet champagne. I didn't even contact James to tell him I was in Sydney. Angela booked a fancy restaurant for dinner. We dressed to the nines and the limo arrived to drive us to Darling Harbour.

When we entered the restaurant the Maître di walked us to our table and to my surprise James was standing at the table waiting for us. He had filled the table with pink roses and balloons. He was so generous. He had organised the whole trip and had even paid for Angela and her partner. That was the best birthday surprise I had ever had in my life or so I thought. After a night of passionate lovemaking, I was awoken by James in the morning asking me to quickly pack my suitcase as he had another surprise for me. He had hired a helicopter to fly us to the Palazzo Versace in Queensland. We spent a whole week there. Needless to say, I was one very spoilt lady that week. James also hired a red Ferrari for the week. He took me sightseeing and shopping and took me to fancy restaurants for dinner and of course, there was dancing. On Valentine's Day, we went for dinner to a restaurant within Palazzo Versace. The restaurant was beautifully decorated. One table had a huge bunch of red roses and a hundred little tea lights. It was so romantic that I was mesmerized.

We were the last two left in the restaurant. After a beautiful meal and many red wines and seeing that no one was in the lobby, we decided to sneak out to the pool. James suggested we go skinny dipping. We were play fighting when suddenly he started caressing my breasts. My nipples hardened as his hands glided over my body. Even though I tried to resist because we were out in the open but he persisted. 'No' was not in his vocabulary. He entered me and we had wild sex and for a split second, I thought that the heavens had opened and I was sitting on a throne.

Unfortunately, the week quickly came to an end and we had to come back to reality. James and I had incredible love between us for four years but unfortunately, he betrayed my trust. He was involved in criminal activities and I disapproved of such activities. It was not the life for me. So, I ended what could have been a lifelong commitment. I told him that I would never speak to him again and if I saw him on the street I would cross the road to the other side. He pursued me by calling me constantly to the point that I ultimately changed my number. He sent me flowers begging me to forgive him.

Seven years later just after my 47th birthday, I was shopping in the city when I heard a voice calling my name. I turned around to see who it was and there was James in a suit holding a briefcase. He looked very handsome; he hadn't changed a bit. He called "Bella", I turned towards him and said that's my name but I crossed the road and kept walking not turning back. I never saw him again.

Chapter Twelve

I attended night school to develop my psychic abilities. My Nonna was also psychic and she had taught me how to use this gift. I have a passion for all metaphysical things. Make no mistake about it, enlightenment is a destructive process. It has nothing to do with becoming better or being happier, it is the crumbling away of untruth, of seeing through the façade of pretence. It is a complete eradication of everything negative.

I attended spiritual classes as I wanted to have a deeper understanding of my being. The key to understanding others is to understand yourself first. God knows how many times I got all dressed up and ready to go out, but my mother-in-law's destructive powerful words stopped me. I ended up being a couch potato, staying in at night and crying myself to sleep. Love ends when you stop caring, hope ends when you stop breathing. I took small steps every day. I believed I was getting stronger because if I took small steps I would land safely on my feet and discover myself once again, otherwise, I would have to depend on other people. Every time I felt that emptiness I felt as if my faith had failed me. All hopes and dreams had gone. I listened to my inner voice that whispered "Hold on" and I just knew that everything was going to be okay.

At that time I would say "My name is Bella, and this is my story. I drowned myself in sorrow behind closed doors. I often called his name and smile knowing that in his own mysterious way, he loved me once. I lie on my couch and hear his footsteps calling my nickname, Min. Leo named me Min, I am home and I did try to make peace. It's always at the back of my mind and many times I feel helpless just like a child waiting for approval. Life is very precious and very short so I break my silly ego and forgive quickly, believe slowly, love truly, laugh loudly and never avoid anything that makes me happy. But most of all I learnt to trust myself so that every little chapter of my life would eventually fall into place.

I am not going to close the book when bad things happen in my life. I will just turn the page and begin a new chapter and every so often my tears would dry. I didn't even say goodbye that night. Going towards the elevator my heart died and I wanted so badly to whisper "Goodbye" in his ear. I felt as though I had died a hundred times in his hands. Mistakes are painful but as time goes by, they become a collection of experiences called lessons. Even though a few years have gone by but I still can't bring myself to tell anyone what really happened between us. I know he is not here anymore, but I feel his presence right here in this house. He really loved this house. I truly believe that he wanted this house very badly and it is now haunted by his restless soul. When we were together, I had no voice and my silence meant I had adapted to the changes in my life.

Leo often comes into my thoughts. Mainly when I am lying down with my eyes closed I can almost see him around me. All the things he put me through bring tears to my eyes and I become overwhelmed with emotion. Lost for words a thousand questions were running through my mind. I sit on the chair with a tear-stained face and a pounding pain in my heart like a sharp knife cutting through my soul. I immediately feel flushed, catching my breath while my heart skips beats. I did not fully understand the effect and the power that this man had over me. All I know is that I fell in love and I didn't want to let him go but at the same time, my body betrayed me. To this day I tremble with fear because I couldn't help myself. I had this weakness for him. I hungered for his touch like a beast with an empty belly. His eyes would just melt my soul. I ache for his touch and long for his kisses. He was my perfect slice of heaven and I couldn't resist him. He was irresistible; he was my life and even though he inflicted pain, I so loved him.

My brain is overloaded with regrets. My heart breaks every time I think of him. It is shattered like broken glass. Once broken, it can never be put back together. I would rather feel everything than feel nothing. I would rather stay soft in this hard world than stay miserable. My heart is not afraid anymore. My head is full of confusion. My heart only knows how to love and how to forgive. I would rather suffer than hurt someone else. My heart only knows how to be kind and how to love even though I am broken. At times when I am in deep thought, I would like to stop time just to love him a little bit longer. But then I feel that my wings were clipped and one day when I am ready to fly I know that I will be okay. Four years have gone by since he left me with a semi-trailer full of scars. I hide my tears when someone mentions your name but the pain in my heart is like a sharp knife. I smile and seem to be carefree but no one misses you more than me.

Leo was a very high force of evil. He wasn't scared of anyone. He was fearless, a loose demon from hell, and I fell right into his trap. I was blindsided by the love I felt for the man. I was so smitten with him that I went through life with a blindfold over my eyes. I refused to even acknowledge that he wasn't a good man. I turned a blind eye even when he was spitting venom. How I loved him but now that he is out of my life, I really miss the man I thought he was, the other half of my heart. I remember so many times begging him on my knees to forgive me for all the things I had not done. My heart still aches when I think of him. I can't get him out of my mind, I really miss the man I once loved but I can never forgive him for all that he did to me.

When I think deeply, I realised I was blamed for everything wrong that happened to him. My scars still bleed to this day. I was blamed for all the mistakes he made. Now it is just a space where all my dreams are lost and time wasted. I forgave him so many times that in the end, I had nothing else left to give. But in my mind, all the good and bad memories are a part of my journey. But one thing was that though I was afraid I was brave. Tomorrow is a new day and my heart is flooded with so many unnecessary tears. The most peaceful heart can also be tormented out of its serenity into a raging inferno that burns the love that one can feel.

A million of my dreams are shattered into pieces and I am left with haunted memories. I was borrowing his happiness and the sorrow was a force of evil. Whenever I think of Leo my heart trembles with fear as I was deeply blinded by the love that I felt for him. I didn't want to believe that this deep love was there to destroy me as I was part of his journey.

Even though it was a very long time ago, I still remember every moment I spent with him. There were so many good and bad memories. When I close my eyes and think of the times we spent together intimately I get a sensual feeling. Even his touch on my hand will remain with me forever. Sometimes when I engage in conversation with the heavens, the tiny pulse deep inside me becomes the sound of drums. I feel that one day my soul will reach out to meet him in the highest of the heavens where he will be judged by God. Then there will be no escape. But now a billion fleeting moments have merged to make a lifetime of precious moments. It is forever. What can I say? My love for Leo was like a hunger that couldn't be satisfied and it returned a million times stronger.

It seems like yesterday when I first saw his smiling face. He looked at me with his beautiful piercing green eyes. Even though years have passed I still dream of him. One night I heard he had got married and of course, his bride had been selected by his mother. She was an 18-year-old virgin. I pretended to be happy for him but my heart was crying. That night I was so restless that I went for a long walk. I went to bed at 9 o'clock but I couldn't get him out of my mind. Finally, I drifted off to sleep.

All in the Name of Love

I dreamt of him that night and he told me he was going to return home late. It was like I knew I had to get a good sleep before he came home. I could hear his voice calling, "Bella, I'm home, I am coming up to bed in a minute". I could feel him lying next to me. I was at the edge of the bed and I thought I would fall off. So, I elbowed him but I didn't feel him next to me anymore. I quickly got up and switched on the light and saw that the quilt on my side of the bed was raised. I wasn't scared. I saw a beautiful guardian angel lying there. I felt my tears flowing like a river and it was like the autumn winds had become cold and the countryside was bleak and bare. It felt as if a storm had come to destroy me. At the same time when I am in deep thought, I can still hear his voice saying, "I am home." I thank God that I am still alive to tell the story.

One cold windy night a friend invited me for dinner. Since she was running late and I was waiting for her to arrive, I ordered a drink. A young man old enough to be my son approached me introducing himself as Leo. He spoke broken English which was very hard to understand. He started talking to me and offered to buy me a drink. I told him that I already had one and thanked him and hoped he would be on his way. He promptly tipped my drink on the floor and said, "Now you don't have one and so I must buy you a drink." We chatted for a while. He had beautiful piercing green eyes and was very charming. He looked straight into my eyes and said, "You are so beautiful." I blushed as it had been a long time since I had been complimented like that. Little did I know at the time that this love affair that was about to begin would nearly end my life.

Finally, my friend arrived and I went out to greet her leaving my bag and phone on the table. While I was gone he quickly put his number into my phone. When I came back, I picked up my phone and bag, thanked him for the drink, and went on to have dinner. After dinner, we moved to another section of the hotel where a band was playing. As I was dancing with my friend, I felt someone dancing close to me. I turned around and it was Leo. I was embarrassed and asked him what he thought he was doing. I left the dance floor. He replied "What?" And I told him that I was old enough to be his mother. He ran after me, grabbing my hand as he said, "You have a problem with your age? You are so beautiful." But I kept walking. My girlfriend followed but I told her I wanted to go home. I bid farewell to my friend and went home. The next day I got up, showered, got dressed, and left for work. When I got to my office, I checked my phone and noticed a new number which I did not remember putting there.

I did not recognize the number but thought it was a client, I called them back after my shift at work. I called the number and said, "Hi! My name is Bella, I saw your number in my phone but I am not sure how it got there". I asked who he was and he told me, "It's me, Leo." I asked "Who?" He replied "Leo". I then asked "How on earth did your number get into my phone?" He replied, "I put it there when you went to meet your friend." I asked, "Why would you do that?" His reply was, "I want to take you out to dinner," I said, "No I am busy, thank you." For the next whole week, every morning he would text to wish me good morning and every night he would text "Goodnight, my princess."

All in the Name of Love

At first, he would not tell me where he was from. He just said Europe, to which I replied Europe is a very large continent. After many text messages and phone calls, I decided to give in and go out for dinner with this man. He asked me where I would like to eat, so to teach him a lesson I picked a very expensive restaurant to prove that he could not afford a woman like me. That day I ordered the most expensive bottle of wine and the most expensive dish on the menu. To my surprise when the bill came, he paid it in full refusing my offer to pay or at least to even pay half. He responded with "I am a European, do not insult me". I dropped him at his car and that was the end of the night. He had tried to kiss me, but I refused his advances. I just said goodnight.

The next day he called me for another dinner date and I replied, "Leo I have a son older than you at home". He replied saying you have no idea how beautiful you are. I am in love with your slim hot body and long blonde hair. You look like you are in your 30's not in your 40's. He kept persisting about dinner but I told him I was busy all week but maybe could be available the following week. On the night we were supposed to meet, I switched off my phone and went out with my girlfriends. Around 11.30 pm I decided to switch on my phone and saw several missed calls and the phone started ringing immediately. I answered and it was Leo. He was very angry and demanded to know where I had been all night. I told him I was out dancing and drinking with my friends. He wanted me to go and meet him, but I said no I just wanted to stay and dance. He wanted to know where I was and when I told him, he was there in no time. He wanted me to go for a drive with him.

As we were driving, I started to panic as we were heading toward the hills near where I lived. He pulled up in front of a house that was only a street away from my house. He asked me if I liked the house. It was absolutely beautiful. He told me that if I liked it he would buy it for me. I said what are you talking about? He said that if I liked it I could have it tomorrow as it belonged to his uncle. He then asked me what area I lived in and if I owned my own home. I replied that I live in a small unit. He then asked me when I was going to invite him for dinner. I said sorry, I can't cook and he said that's ok because he was a chef and would cook for me. I started laughing. He pulled over and tried to kiss me, but I asked him to stop, stop, stop, as I was not ready for a relationship. I pushed him away even though I was liking all the attention he was giving me.

That night he was a real gentleman and treated me like a princess. From the moment I had laid eyes on him, I knew deep down that he was different. There was something about him that I just couldn't pinpoint. I found Leo very exciting but there was a little voice in my head which was screaming danger. Leo made me feel everything so intensely but there was something about him that gave me warning signs. This was the reason I wanted to get to know him more. As crazy as this was, I knew I had strong feelings for him. I knew I would probably regret this, but I wanted to get to know him better. For the next three months, we met at clubs and bars and had dinners together. Finally, I invited him to my house. I had also invited a few friends over to play pool and eat pizza. When he came through my door his mouth dropped. He said, I thought you lived in a small place, whose house is this? I replied that it was mine.

He was all over me that night and it made me uncomfortable in front of my friends. One of them even commented, "Get a room". Everyone left around 2 am but Leo stayed. I had had a few too many wines and he asked where the bedroom was. I told him upstairs and he carried me up the stairs and the whole night we had wild sex. At 9 am he told me to shower and get dressed because he wanted to take me for breakfast to Hahndorf. We spent the day together and that night he stayed over again for another night of passion.

On Monday morning I showered and was getting ready for work when he asked if he could stay at my house all day. I told him no. I told him to get up and have a shower because he had to leave. He argued that he could stay and would cook dinner for me. Again I answered no you must leave. He got upset, got dressed, and left saying that I'll be seeing you. While I was at work, I received a message saying, "Hi beautiful, why did you ask me to leave? I wanted to stay and cook dinner for you. You know you love me; you know you want to be with me as much as I want to be with you."

Six months passed by and we not only saw a lot of each other but did many things together. That's when he started asking me for a key to my house. He told me he loved me. But I thought how can you love someone that you have just met? I didn't know him, but I thought that is how the new generation behaved. I really did like him, but I wasn't in love with him. Maybe I had been on my own for too long but when I was with him

I longed for his touch and his kisses. The desire would become a fire, the love became life, my body melted into his and he fulfilled all my fantasies. Never in my wildest dreams did I ever expect to end up with someone a lot younger than me.

Finally, I gave in and gave him the key to my house. I kept telling myself that I couldn't miss this opportunity. He was an amazing, gorgeous guy who treated me like a princess. He was always there for me and he was the perfect man for me. However, as time went by, I got to know the real him. I discovered he was not Italian, he was Albanian. He had no house, just a rusty old bomb of a car and a garbage bag of dirty clothes. Although he was unbelievable in bed, I still had my doubts. He would act like my house was his. Things changed between us, but he was quite comfortable in my house and started setting rules though I still believed that he was a good person. On Valentine's Day, I received a beautiful box of 12 red roses, each one had my name written in gold and we had dinner at a very fancy restaurant. He wasn't working so I couldn't understand how he could afford all this. On my birthday he took me out for a surprise birthday dinner. I reminded myself about how lucky I was.

A couple of days later I received my phone bill which was higher than usual. I let it go but when the next phone bill came it was triple what it normally would be, so I asked who he was calling as the bill was so high. He replied that he was calling his mother and brothers overseas. One day I came home to an empty house and Leo was nowhere to be seen. I pressed the recall button on the house phone. A young woman answered. I asked her if she could speak English and she answered that she could speak Albanian and Italian. I asked her if she knew Leo. She said yes, he is my husband-to-be. We've been together since high school, and we're engaged to be married. She asked me who I was and I told her I was his girlfriend. She said no he is with an old woman only for a visa to stay in the country and that he is not sleeping with her.

I stayed very calm and told her we are girlfriend and boyfriend and are living together. She called me a slut and said he would not do anything like that. I then called Leo and asked him to come home immediately, but it took him six hours as he was with his friends and couldn't leave. When he finally came home, I told him what I had done and had spoken to his supposed fiancé. All he could say in his defence was that he felt sorry for her and let her believe he would marry her. I told him either he calls her that instant in front of me and tell her it was over and that he would not marry her or he would have to leave my home immediately. He was very apologetic for what he had done. He rang her and told her he was not going to marry her and that his life was with me. The following year he was the perfect partner and we were inseparable doing everything together. We were very happy or so I thought.

The next day I got out of bed, had a coffee, and went off to work. That afternoon when I returned home from work, I found Leo sitting under the gazebo having a cigarette. I ran up to him and gave him a huge kiss. Leo said "You know Min we have been together for three years and I would like to take you away for a week to Melbourne for the Melbourne Cup race. I was so happy

I started jumping for joy like a little schoolgirl. I had never attended the Melbourne Cup but it was always on my bucket list of things to do. Leo asked me to start packing as we were leaving on Sunday.

Chapter Thirteen

After three blessed years of being together during which time Leo never had a job, but his pockets were never empty. He always had an abundance of money. I never questioned him. From the beginning of our relationship, Leo had rules. One of them was that I could not ask questions. I never once asked where or how he was getting his money.

One morning I told Leo it's my day off today, get dressed and I will shout you breakfast. He replied, "Of course honey". As we were finishing our breakfast a very gruff and rough-looking man came towards us and shook Leo's hand. They knew each other and they spoke Albanian. Leo said to me "Honey, I have to go somewhere, take the keys and go home".

On the way back to the car I spotted a lingerie shop. I spoiled myself and bought not one but three sets of stunning lingerie - One white, one black, and one red with suspenders. Then I went into a florist shop and bought a large bunch of beautiful pink tulips. It was a warm day and as soon as I got home I took my lingerie upstairs and grabbed a quick shower. I couldn't resist trying them on. I put on the white set with the lace G-string. It looked amazing and I threw on a beautiful, pleated baby doll dress. I wanted to look good for my toy boy. I went back downstairs and picked up a crystal vase to put my tulips into. I heard the door open. Leo saw me and grabbed me, lifted me into his arms, and said, "You look good enough to eat". I giggled. He said you look like a million dollars baby. I asked him to put me down and sit down and close his eyes. "I have a surprise for you, no peeking, ok?" He closed his eyes and I dropped my dress. He opened his eyes and said, "Oh God, Min". I asked him "What do you think"? Leo said, "You look better than any 20-year-old. I am a very lucky man to have you". He sat me on the breakfast bar, then pulled my G-string off and started caressing my hot spot with his tongue. That afternoon the sex was mind-blowing.

It was a warm night and that evening about 8 pm we went to the beach for a walk. As we were walking it got dark and I said to him "Let's sit here for a while". We sat and watched the waves with the moonlight bouncing off the water. I was sitting between his legs leaning against him and his arms were wrapped tightly around me. He suddenly lifted me and sat me onto a rock, pulled my bathers aside, and urgently pushed his penis into me. It was a very precious moment with his perfect motions and the sound of the waves crashing.

Finally, Sunday arrived and we were waiting for a taxi to take us to the airport, but I got a surprise as a big black stretch limousine arrived. Leo said that the limousine was taking us to Melbourne. He had organised a beautiful surprise. We had a bottle of Moet Chandon champagne in beautiful crystal champagne glasses. On the way to Melbourne Leo said he had another surprise for me and hoped I would like it. Leo removed his tie and placed it over my eyes as a blindfold. He asked me to hold out my hand and he put something into it. I started giggling and asked him what is in here. He said something that he hoped would make me very happy. "Min, you are the most beautiful thing that I have ever laid eyes on and I don't care who you have been with in the past as I want to be your last. You take my breath away; you are my everything, but I want to be your last everything. From this moment on you are my wife, with your permission." He was so raw and honest. I asked him if I could remove my blindfold. He said of course. When I opened my eyes, I smiled and said, "What's this?" "Open it". I was very excited but also nervous. I opened the small box. What a surprise, it was a huge diamond ring. I quickly closed the box. Leo asked me if I was ok. I said, Oh my god." At first, I thought I was seeing things and I exclaimed, "What a huge diamond ring! Oh my goodness, how could you afford this?" He said nothing was too much for his future wife. I replied this must be a dress ring as it couldn't be real. He said, "No Min, if you accept this very real ring then from today on we are married."

I said "Okay", and he said, "Anything for you since you are my everything. Before you came along, I was all alone. Then you came into my life and not only did you welcome me into your home, but you never stopped loving me for a minute and now I am complete. I love you so much." I replied "You are my everything too. You take my breath away. I love you and my heart and spirit belong to you." He quickly closed the window of the limousine. We kissed passionately and Leo was aroused and placed my hand on his crutch. He said "Look what you have done to me. With the other hand, he picked up his champagne flute and took a mouthful. He came towards my lips to kiss me and as I opened my mouth he emptied a mouthful of champagne into my mouth. He grabbed me and I asked him to take it easy or he would rip my Camilla silk dress. Leo started undressing me slowly and gently. I was wearing my black lace body suit. He tied my hands above my head with his tie and he proceeded to make love to me on the way to Melbourne. It was a ride I will never forget.

Finally, after almost eight hours of driving we arrived in Melbourne. We stayed at the Hilton Hotel. The next morning we went downstairs into the restaurant for breakfast and then proceeded to meet with another couple not far from the Hotel. Leo's friend looked like a gangster. He was very well-dressed and groomed. Leo introduced me to this gentleman and his wife Jill. We had coffee together. The men were engrossed in their own conversation, so I started talking to his wife and asked her what her husband did for a living. She replied, "He isn't really my husband. Don't tell anyone but I am getting paid to marry him." I asked in surprise "What do you mean?" I was very confused by her statement. She then proceeded to tell me how he was paying her to marry him so he could get his visa. He was paying her half of $80,000 when they marry and the other half once he received his citizenship. I was shocked. She then went on to tell me that on paper he was a painter, but he hasn't worked a day since she met him.

After some time we all proceeded to the races. I couldn't understand how familiar Leo was with this man.

All in the Name of Love

I thought it was strange that I had never heard Leo talk about him.

Leo excused himself to go to the amenities and the man went with him. The Cup was almost over so I texted Leo "What happened to you? Are you ok?" He texted back "I just bumped into a friend; I'll be there soon". In the meantime, while I was waiting for him someone approached me and asked if I would like to participate in the fashion parade for the best dressed. I quickly texted Leo to get his approval. He replied, "Yes, of course". I ended up winning the fashion parade but still Leo was nowhere to be seen. I kept myself busy as there was so much happening around me. Finally, he showed up at 6 pm, very apologetic. He told me he had lost track of time. He asked me if my horse won. I started laughing and replied no mine is still running and yours? He responded "You are going to be so proud of me, Gorgeous, I won $50,000. Jokingly I said "What are you going to buy me?" He said, "Whatever your heart desires."

The next morning, we went for breakfast in Charleston, and all his men were waiting for him. It looked like a scene from one of the Sicilian gangster movies. We all had breakfast together and as usual, they were speaking in their language. I didn't understand anything that was being said. I thought it was very rude. About an hour later Leo excused himself and we went off. We went into a Gucci shop and he pointed to a gorgeous white gold Gucci bracelet. The assistant placed the bracelet on my wrist. I instantly fell in love with it. Leo didn't even ask for the price, he just told me to leave it on and that he will pay for it. We then went to the Louis Vuitton gift shop and Leo bought me a beautiful handbag. I was extremely happy.

We caught a taxi to Melbourne and started walking towards the Casino. As we were approaching the Casino we bumped into Jill and her husband, the painter. Jill asked me when Leo and I were going back to Adelaide and I told her tomorrow morning. They asked us to have lunch together, but first Leo and I went back to the hotel room to drop off our shopping. We met with them and had a leisurely lunch together. Jill mentioned that she and her husband were going to Adelaide tomorrow as well and would we like to travel back with them? Leo said of course, we would love to.

A week after the Melbourne Cup on a Saturday night Leo said to me in the morning, "I am taking you to Enzo's restaurant." I was pleasantly surprised. Wrapping his arms around me, he responded "Nothing but the best for my wife". I felt truly blessed. That evening we arrived at Enzo's and as we were about to sit down we noticed the couple from Melbourne. I informed Leo. He came over to our table and Leo greeted him with a handshake. They had a table for six and insisted that we join them.

The waiter walked us to their table and boy, did they have a surprise for me. As we were exchanging a few words two very well-dressed young men came up to the table. One was called Andrea. The young 22-year-old sat next to me and I noticed he had an exclusive Rolex watch on his wrist for which I complimented him. He was very polite and said thank you. He spoke broken English. We started chatting and he asked me what I did. I responded, "I am a psychic and you?" He proceeded to tell me that he was a painter; we made a joke out of it. He told me he was in a little bit of trouble. I asked him what kind of trouble, and he asked me if I would write a letter for him declaring that he was insane. He needed to put it before a judge so hopefully, he won't go to jail. I need to see you, please book me an appointment. I told him it would be best if he would see someone else. He insisted that he wanted to come to me. Grudgingly, I gave him the phone number for the practice.

I told him that he needed a referral from a GP otherwise I won't be able to see him. I don't know how but he got an appointment for Monday afternoon. He told me why he was going up before a judge. "You see Bella, I had sent a suitcase to Melbourne which contained $15,000 cash. I flew to Melbourne a day earlier. When I went to collect the suitcase I was arrested at the airport." I excused myself and said, "Where do I fit into this story?" He said, "Please write me a letter declaring my insanity." I said "I am not doing that as I can lose my job and it's against the law. I could end up going to jail." I was so disappointed with Leo and said to myself "What a disgusting man to set me up for disaster". I changed the subject and then Jill replied, "You could help him just this once?" Her husband responded with "Shut your mouth. Do I need to remind you who the boss is?" She replied, "No I didn't forget I remember everything". As we got up to leave, I said to the young guy "Sorry, I can't help you".

On the drive home, Leo was very quiet. When we got home his phone rang. I could hear snippets of the conversation, "Stop stressing, leave it up to me, I will sort it out".

I quickly went to bed and Leo followed me. I started yelling at him that how could he set me up like that? I could lose my job and not be able to practice again. Leo remained calm and said, "Listen to me for a moment. He is young and handsome. Do you have any idea what they are going to do to him in jail? His mother died when he was a child, he is all alone. He has got himself into a little bit of trouble and you are the only person who could help him, Min. Please do it for your gorgeous". This was a nickname Leo had given himself. "I know you will do it for me. Just this once help him as he is struggling with his personal demons." I told Leo that I would see what I can do. Leo held me tight all night and I felt blessed that he truly loved me.

I woke up in the morning with Leo's arms wrapped around me. I got out of bed without waking him up. The previous night was playing on my mind. I was sitting in the sunroom and staring at my beautiful engagement ring, feeling truly grateful. I was looking outside at the beautiful blue skies with the shining Sun. The view from this room was breathtaking and I was sitting in one of my favourite chairs. When I looked out I could see the top of the gum trees. It's as if one could almost touch heaven. It was 24 degrees, a magical day. I could see lorikeet birds eating together in peace and harmony sucking on the gum tree flowers. It was like watching the perfect slice of heaven, free as the wind, free as a bird about to fly, free as a bumble bee's freedom that the whole world cried for.

Ultimately, Leo convinced me to write the letter and also got a psychiatrist to write a letter saying he was not mentally sound. I was prepared to go to court in Melbourne to testify that he was taking a lot of medication and was not thinking straight. Then I arranged for him to see a psychiatrist so he could get a letter from him as well. I schooled him so he knew exactly what to say to the psychiatrist. Andrea got his court date for a month later. He took a photo of the board with his name on it and sent it to me. He wanted me to wish him good luck. I wished him good luck and said if you need me you know my number.

One day, I had a very busy afternoon and my phone was sitting silently on my desk. Suddenly, my phone started flashing and I quickly answered the call. It was Andrea, he was so happy and jumping up and down with joy. He had got six months for good behaviour. Three months later he got caught in Queensland with a large quantity of cocaine. It was all over the news. The street value of the same was almost a million dollars. When Leo came home that evening, he didn't mention anything to me at all. I asked him, "Have you seen the news? They have arrested your friend". Leo played dumb and went for a shower. I didn't mention it again.

A month later Andrea was once again in the news. Security was escorting him onto a plane to deport him back to his hometown, Thrusher. I asked Leo where would Andrea live when he returned home. Leo responded, "He has a mansion and plenty of money, he has his parents and family". My jaw dropped, "You told me he didn't have a mother". "I lied to you. Anyway, he won't be going to jail when he gets there. We rule the jails over there". He turned to me and said "If you treat me like a king one day I will show you how the game is played." I replied, "Leave me out of this shit from now on." Leo started raising his voice to me saying "You should be ashamed of yourself. For someone who has been living in Australia for so many years you don't have much, just this house."

Chapter Fourteen

About a year later, one day out of the blue Leo's brother and sister-in-law knocked at my front door and told me they were moving in with us for six months as if they owned me. Leo had invited them to live with us without telling me. His sister-in-law and I hit it off and became the best of friends and his brother had a lot of respect for me. We took them all over Australia to show them our beautiful country. We all got along very well. One day when I was at work, during my lunch break I noticed I had 10 missed calls from Leo. I panicked as I thought something bad had happened. Instead, he just wanted me to come home straight from work as his other brother and sister-in-law had just arrived from Albania and he wanted me to cook for them. I was so angry, but I didn't let on.

Once I finished cooking for all of them I went and sat outside under the gazebo crying my eyes out. Not one person came out to see if I was ok. They all left after dinner and I started cleaning up. They also moved in with us unannounced, but unlike the first couple, they came across as nice but in fact they were very nasty and troublesome. Things quickly changed. The women had to stay at home to cook and clean but the men went out every night and we weren't allowed to ask where.

One afternoon I got a phone call from Leo telling me to get ready as we were all going out for dinner. He came and picked me up and off we went. As he was driving the phone kept ringing and it was annoying him. Once we got to the place he pulled over and asked me to walk into the restaurant as he had to park the car. I understood that he wanted privacy to take the call as he didn't want me to listen. I waited for a good 10 minutes. The usher took us to the table where Leo's brothers were already seated and the food had started arriving. I greeted his brothers. They all stood up and went to say hello to someone.

Leo left his phone on the table and I saw a message come through saying, "What time are you coming over tonight? I will be in the bath waiting and will leave the door open". I quickly took a photo of the message with my phone and entered the phone number into my phone. He received another text and I put that number also into my phone. When I had a chance, I rang up both numbers telling the girls that I was Leo's girlfriend. They were not happy, to say the least. But this didn't stop Leo from finding another woman. Voula called me and told me she was Leo's lover. She wanted to know who I was. She told me that her name was Voula and she was a Greek lady who was marrying an Albanian for lots of money. A set-up marriage. But in the end, he cooked himself in his own juice.

When Christmas came around that year, I realised that their traditions were nothing like mine. I had my family for lunch but instead of them talking to my family they chose to speak amongst themselves in their language and excluded my family. As soon as lunch was over, my family left as they felt very uncomfortable. My family also felt that their laughter and jokes were aimed at them. On New Year's Eve Leo and I went out for dinner with his family and as usual, they spoke in their language and I just sat there because I didn't understand one word of what they were saying. I was told we were going to Glenelg to watch the fireworks, but I was not allowed to walk beside my partner, I had to walk three feet behind him. At midnight also I was not allowed to kiss my partner, I could only shake his hand. We got home around 1 am, but the men went out clubbing and we girls went to bed. They did not get home till 7 am and no questions could be asked.

I did not understand what was going on as my partner had not been like this before his brothers had arrived. We used to do everything together. But when his eldest brother arrived Leo changed. That day they finally got up around 2 pm and Leo, his brothers, and their wives went to visit some fellow country friends. I was not invited and had to stay home alone which upset me a lot. I was told I was not allowed to go as I did not understand their language. At around 7 pm Leo called me to tell me to put dinner on the table as they were on their way home. I felt like I was his slave. His family always praised my cooking. After dinner, I excused myself and went to bed. The next morning I was up early and feeling very sorry for myself. I was drinking my coffee outside under my gazebo and crying when I noticed his younger brother in the kitchen. I quickly dried my eyes, but he realized that something was wrong and asked me to tell him. But I just said that there was nothing wrong.

My life of being left out and disrespected continued for another six months. After that one brother and his wife went back to their homeland, but the other brother made me feel very uneasy in my own house. His wife was very shy and sneaky. They were a very unusual couple. From day one I had felt that I was being used. They were always crawling up my arse like a pair of underpants. Some crawl up, some snap under pressure, some don't have the strength to hold you up, some get twisted, some are your favourites, some support you, some are cheap and nasty and get bent out of shape and some actually cover your arse when you need them to.

I was always burning sage to remove the bad energy in my home. After three months of being in Australia, the couple was always making demands as if they owned me. Leo's brother lost all his licence points for speeding. They demanded that I give him two of my points. To do this I had to go in front of a justice of peace. I was sitting down filling the forms and where it asked for colour of the eyes, I wrote brown. I was told by him that isn't the way to write brown. I felt like telling the truth to the JP but instead pretended to be stupid as if I didn't know anything. I kept silent but, on the inside, I was really angry. Clearly, his communication skills were absolutely zero. There were no two ways about it, this couple was only looking out for themselves and nothing else mattered to them.

When I finally got home, I sat down for a minute and started thinking about my Nonna, and all of a sudden what she used to say came into my mind, "Never be afraid to raise your voice for honesty, truth, justice, and greed. If people do not try to correct a fool, he will hate you, but sweetheart, don't be afraid to correct a wise man as he will appreciate it. Do everything with a good heart and expect nothing in return and you will never be disappointed". Leo had invited his brother and sister-in-law to live with us without telling me. His sister-in-law was pure evil and quite content to keep living for free in my home. I couldn't take this anymore and so I told him and his wife that they had to find their own home.

This didn't go down well with Leo or his brother. I found a house for them and finally they moved out. Taking them in and having them in my home at no expense to them was never appreciated and once they moved out Leo would go to their house for dinner every week, but I was never invited. This did not bother Leo, and I was realising day-by-day that he was not the same person I had met. I was very unhappy and one day I confronted him. We had a huge argument and then he became violent and shouted, "You wanted to be an Albanian, this is how an Albanian woman gets treated." He punched me in the face, my vision became blurred and I ended up with two black eyes.

Then he threw me against the wall and watched as I slid down covered in cracked plaster. Not finished, he approached me with a crazed look in his darkening eyes and grabbed a fistful of my hair, ripping out chunks of my golden locks. Although weak, I tried to fight him off but I was overpowered by his stature. A final blow to my already bruised and bloodied face was all it took to finally knock me out. Succumbing to the darkness wasn't even frightening, rather it was the darkness that I ached and longed to fall into.

Ice cold water drowning my senses pulled me out of the peace I was feeling, bringing me back to the reality I had never imagined in my tormented sleep. Having come back to reality, I managed to climb the stairs to the bathroom. Looking into the mirror, the woman I saw looking back at me was no more than a shell of the person I was; broken and destroyed. Moving to the shower, I slowly let the warm water run over my black and blue body. The water soothed my aching muscles but stung the skin which was littered with cuts and now forming bruises. The shower might have eased the bleeding but it definitely did not mend my shattered soul. Getting dressed was a struggle but I managed to do so without uttering a sound. Before long he entered the room which instantly turned cold. The chill I felt in my arms was frightening as I knew he had come to the bedroom to watch me struggle, observing his handy work with a proud glint in his eyes.

After my shower, I got dressed and waited for him to go out before calling his brother. When I spoke to his brother, he just said, "Well, what can you do? He needs to grow up." He was not at all sympathetic to me. So, I called a dear friend of mine, Monica, and told her what had happened. She immediately came over and when I opened the door she was beside herself with anger. She started crying and hugging me and wanted me to report him to the police, but I couldn't as he had threatened he would kill members of my family. He had also threatened me that he would take me to Coober Pedy and drop me into a mine shaft where no one would ever find me, not even the police. He told me he had mental health issues and would go to the doctors and make up stories and even spend time in a mental institution if he got into trouble. He would tell the authorities that he was not responsible for his actions. He often threatened me with this saying he wouldn't go to jail even if he killed me. I was scared for myself and my family and I didn't know what to do.

I started to realize what kind of a man he was. He believed that a woman should not be heard and should obey the man in her life. Women should be submissive, cook food, do the housework, and never go out, but men could go out, have affairs, drink, gamble and do whatever they liked. He drank a lot, the more he drank the more violent he became. He even told me he would chop me up. Time and again he also said that my house was his and not mine and so, what he said goes. I started keeping a journal of everything he did to me and told my friend Monica that should I disappear or if I died and I would not take my own life, then I have a journal hidden and told her where she would find it to give to the police. I was petrified of him and became his maid not his partner. I could not even get him to move out of my house.

I tried to make the best of the situation so as not to upset him or I would be punished. If I did not do or say what he asked his reaction would be putting his hands around my neck and saying you know where your place is and would point to the balcony and tell me that he would throw me off. One day we had a disagreement over money which he did not have. He got so angry that he picked me up and lay me on the balcony rail. With one hand he held me down and the other hand was over my mouth, threatening to throw me over if I screamed. Ultimately, I had to apologise to him, so he would let me down. He often said you know one day I will kill you.

I will relate an incident just to give you some insight into what kind of a person Leo was. On one occasion I received a phone call from a girlfriend of mine. It was winter and her car had broken down. She told me she was at her mother's house and asked me to come over and that her mother would also love to see me after so long. She had a little whinge saying that since I was with Leo, I didn't make time for my friends anymore. My girlfriend was very ill with diabetes and kidney disease. She put me on the phone with her mother. She made me feel very guilty so I tried calling Leo, but his phone was switched off. I decided to go as it was not far from my home. I stayed with them for a couple of hours and around 10 pm I said I needed to go home. My girlfriend asked if I would drive her home and I said of course. She was very weak. All of a sudden, a car with a siren was behind me so I pulled over. I panicked as I had already received a fine the previous week and I thought I would definitely lose my licence this time. I pulled over and I could see a gentleman walk towards my side of the car and he knocked on my window. I was shocked to see that it was Leo. I said to him "What the heck? When did you become a police officer?" He noticed my girlfriend was in the car so he just said, "I will see you at home" and walked back to his car and drove off.

When I got home, I poured myself a stiff drink of scotch and sat near the fire thinking about what had happened. Leo arrived home and kissed me on the lips. I said very nicely, "I didn't know you were a police officer?" And he replied, "There are a lot of things you don't know about me. You cannot tell anyone what happened tonight." He was very frank when he said this to me. I said, "You have a very flashy car for a cop." He then proceeded to tell me that he was an undercover cop. He gave me some spiel about having 10 fake licenses. I had been so embarrassed and kept wondering what my girlfriend thought. I sat back and thought that he was really making my life unbearable. He was capable of anything. He had no conscience. He had tried to kill me on so many occasions. I was stuck in an abusive relationship. He was unemployed but he acted like a big shot at my expense. I was forced to support the man who treated me so unfavourably. I feared living in my own home. In my heart, I knew that the man I had fallen in love with was being controlled by his evil brother and if I didn't do as I was told, he would kill me.

On another occasion, Leo and his brothers got dressed up in their suits and they all looked like gangsters. One of his brother's wives went upstairs to ask her husband if she could go out with them. Suddenly, I heard a scream. I ran upstairs and saw that she was crying. I could see the imprint of a hand on her cheek. When I asked her if she was alright her husband told me to go back downstairs.

One morning I made coffee for everybody. The evil brother wanted me to pour his coffee into one of my Versace cups. I did as he asked. I went to bring Leo his coffee and asked him why his brother suddenly wanted to have his coffee in the Versace cups and his response was "Because he can, this is his house". He slapped me on my face.

On another occasion, Leo came home and asked me to write out a cheque for $3,000. Since I didn't have that kind of money on me, we got into an argument. He asked me into the garage and drew a gun and put it to my head. Then he pushed me into the cellar and slammed the door shut. He said, "If you make any noise, I swear I will shoot you tonight". I was trembling with fear and thought I was going to die and wet myself. He came home in the early hours of the morning. He came to open the cellar door and said "See what happens when you don't obey me. I am the boss of this house and you have lost that privilege. I didn't meet you accidentally. I knew everything about you, I knew you had money". I replied, "Yes you are right, I am truly blessed". My hands were shaking and I was trembling with fear. He said, "Min you know I am going to kill you sooner or later". I thanked my lucky stars that he hadn't killed me yet. After that, he let me out of the cellar.

One evening Leo came home drunk and fell asleep very quickly. He was snoring loudly. I went downstairs, picked up a sharp pointed knife, and went back upstairs to his bedroom. I placed the point of the knife on his throat. He moved and the knife scratched his neck. But luckily it didn't wake him. I quickly ran downstairs and put away the knife. In the morning when he woke up, he noticed the scratch on his neck. He called me and said, "I must have gotten into a fight last night." I just played dumb and went back downstairs. In my head, I was saying, "You are lucky I didn't kill you last night."

Two weeks later on a Friday night, he came home at about 3 am. When he switched on the light, I noticed his hair was all messed up and I could smell that he had been with another woman. As usual, I just lay there pretending that everything was ok. He thought I was asleep, but I was very much awake. As he was about to lie down his phone started vibrating. He was answering a text message and because his English was poor, he nudged me saying, "Bella, how do you spell Princess?" so I spelt it for him. His phone started ringing and he asked me to go to another bedroom. Though I was fuming, I went into another room as requested by him. I wanted to use the bathroom in the ensuite. Leo didn't hear me coming as I was as quiet as a mouse. I looked into the bedroom and saw that he was kneeling on the bed masturbating and holding the phone in the other hand while this woman was watching him. I wanted to say something, but I knew he would hit me and I didn't want to provoke him.

Chapter Fifteen

I started confiding in one of my co-workers and it made me feel much better. She offered me a healing session and while she was healing me she begged me to be very careful and to report him to the cops. Leo guessed that I was confiding in someone so one day when he was pulling my hair he yelled, "One day I will kill you and I will get away with it". I lost my temper and said to him "No you won't get away with it. I have spoken to my co-worker about how abusive you are so you will not get away with killing me". I grabbed my handbag and went off to work. He was still yelling after me "Come back here, you are as good as dead". I felt safe at work. I dreaded going back home. I finished at 5 pm and came home and cooked dinner for him because I knew it was in my best interest.

After dinner, he started yelling again "I am going to teach you a lesson". I had no idea what he was going to do next. Just then his phone started ringing. He started speaking Albanian. He was telling the person on the phone, "I have to go somewhere, I am gonna fix your co-worker" and he went off. The next day I went to work as usual but when I arrived there were a couple of police officers talking to my boss. As I walked in,

I asked the secretary "What happened?" She replied that someone had shot three bullets into the window. I replied, "Was anyone hurt?" and she replied "No, it happened during the night. Thank God no one was hurt." Deep in my heart I knew it was Leo, but I didn't want to believe that he was capable of doing such a despicable thing. My heart was pounding with fear.

When I got home, I confronted him about what had happened at work. He didn't admit that he was responsible. I said to Leo that I am sure the cops will find the guilty. Once again, his response was "Shut the fuck up". I went and sat down for a short while. After a few minutes, he asked me for a few thousand dollars. As predicted when I said sorry I don't have any money, he got very angry and started pacing the kitchen floor. I was sitting on the couch. He pointed a gun at my head and I thought that this was it, he was going to kill me. I stayed very still and wet myself. He yelled at me and told me to stand up and walk to the garage. I had to again go down the stairs and get into the cellar. Leo pushed me to the floor and I hit my head and started bleeding. There were no lights in the cellar, but I could feel the blood running down my face.

Leo locked me in the cellar and I could hear him driving off. I was so thankful that I was still breathing. I must have drifted off to sleep because when I gained consciousness I could hear the garage door open. Leo came to let me out and said, "Get up Bella and make me a coffee." As I was walking towards the light, I could see blood all over my dress. Leo saw it too and told me to have a shower first. "You look like you are having your period and have bled all over your dress." I yelled and said "You pushed me and I hit my head in the cellar. Can't you see the lump and scrape on my forehead?" He said, "You will be alright." I walked past him, but I wasn't sure what he was going to do next. I had to take a week off from work so the bruising could heal.

Leo had houses around Adelaide where he grew crops of marijuana. One of Leo's houses got broken into and his crop was stolen. So, Leo and his brother quickly removed all the equipment from this house and moved it into my garage. I was angry, but I couldn't say anything.

One Saturday I had a hairdressing appointment and my hairdresser commented, "What happened to your head?" I responded, "Please do not ask". She knew better than to pursue the topic as she knew I was with an Albanian. Monday arrived and I was honestly glad to go back to work. First, so I could have time away from Leo, and second because I needed the money. The day went by very fast and it was almost time to finish work for the day when I heard a knock at the door. It was the Secretary.

She said you have one more client. "No, I don't. I have finished all my clients." "Bella, you need to see this woman as she is in a bad state". I relented and she let the woman into my office. The woman looked very fragile and was very oddly dressed. She wore an interesting but beautiful hat. She seemed very simple but I treat my clients with the utmost respect. The woman looked really defeated and started telling me her problems. My heart went out to her and I asked her to tell me a little about herself.

Then she told me that she had had a nervous breakdown and she has no family or friends. I asked her if she was married and she told me that someone took her husband away from her. I also asked her his name. She said "All I know is I took him back twice. He did the same thing to me two times" and then she started crying. I asked her how she had come to my workplace and she said that she had to catch two buses to reach. I then asked her how she found me and she said, "On the internet". I spent about an hour and a half with her and it was time to finally end the conversation. I told her that I would like to see her in two weeks. She left and I went to grab my bag. Suddenly, the heavens opened and it started raining so hard that one could barely see the road. I saw the same woman standing in the rain like a frozen statue. I called her by her name but she didn't respond as she was caught up in her thoughts. I went up to her and shook her and asked "How are you getting home? Is someone picking you up?" She said, "No, no one is picking me up". I told her to get into my car and that I will take her home.

Two weeks passed and she returned to see me at my workplace. She recalled how I had worked long hours and so had brought a hot pasty for me to eat. I thanked her as they were my favourite. She replied, "When you came up to me in the rain that day, I saw a beautiful Angel behind you. The Angel was telling me that he was an Angel of God and that I was going to be fine. Have a little faith in me. May God bless you in every breath you take. Believe and He will always be by your side. God has a master plan for each one of us".

We became good friends and she welcomed me into her life with open arms. She got back on her feet and now has a full-time job and she even writes short stories.

I started confiding in her about Leo and what was happening in my life. I told her about the shooting and how I didn't feel safe anywhere. She sat there in shock and wanted me to explain the shooting. I told her that I had turned up at work one morning and police officers were talking to the staff. Someone had driven past during the night and fired three shots into the front window. I knew in my heart that it was Leo, but I couldn't say any such thing as I didn't want to bear the brunt of my telling and I didn't want my colleagues to know what was going on in my personal life. After the shooting, I didn't feel safe so she gave me a filing cabinet with a key so I could keep my confidential papers in there. I gave her my friend Monica's phone number in case something happened to me. Monica was to be the point of contact. I told her that he was dangerous, but she stood by me and helped me in any way she could.

Here I was so frightened for my life but Leo was living the high life, the best that money could buy. He had impeccable taste. He even bought himself a Rolex. He was making so much money but unfortunately, he was blowing away a lot of it on prostitutes and drugs. He was so proud of himself. He was coming and going as he pleased with no questions asked.

One evening while I was cooking dinner there was a knock on my door. There were three detectives with a search warrant. They started searching my house and asked me if I knew where Leo was and I told them the truth that I didn't know where he was. I never knew where he was. Luck was on his side that evening as they didn't find anything in the house.

The next morning I made him his coffee like I did every day and noticed that he hadn't been home for long. He had a black bag full of gold and I asked him "Where did you get this from?" He said that he had decided to invest in gold. I just rolled my eyes and walked away. When I returned home in the evening he was nowhere to be seen. Leo had been arrested and of course, he had a lawyer, the best that money could buy. Six hours later he was out.

One day, I received a phone call from a Greek woman who told me she was in love with Leo and that he loved her little boy. I asked her where she had got my number from and she said from Leo's phone. She said why do you keep ringing him? I said, "What are you talking about, he lives with me". She then said "Oh you are the old lady who is doing the papers for him." I again asked her who she was and I was trying to stay very calm. She replied, "I am his girlfriend" and I wished her all the best. I was so relieved.

On the weekend Leo asked me to get his clothes ready and he insisted on wearing his Versace coat that evening. It wasn't even cold, but he still insisted. When he returned that evening, I asked him where his coat was and he told me that he had lent it to a friend. Later I discovered that he had given it to the Greek lady, his lover. All that time he lived in my house and never once offered to pay for anything and refused to leave.

But I found out that he paid an Albanian woman who lived in America to come to Adelaide. He collected her from the airport with his brother and his cousin in my BMW four-wheel drive. They took her out for dinner at the best place in town. The next day they all went on a holiday to Queensland. He took his latest lover to have a good time. He spent over $50,000 in seven days. He took her everywhere, hired a Ferrari, went on helicopter flights, and even stayed at the Palazzo Versace Hotel. Never once did he pick up the phone to say he had arrived safely. As usual, it was like I never existed, not that I cared.

When Leo was away, I invited my friend Monica for pizza and a bottle of Moet Chandon. She was more than happy to spend some quality time with me. As we were about to sit down to eat the pizza my phone started ringing. It was the Greek girlfriend begging me not to hang up on her. I asked her what she wanted and she queried if I had heard from Leo as she was worried because Leo wasn't answering her phone calls. I replied sorry, but he is in Queensland with his new Albanian lover. I kept very calm and wished her the best of luck. But deep in my heart and after all the horrible things the man had put me through I was relieved that I had a little time of my own.

However, seven days went by very quickly and before I knew it his brother was pulling up in front of my house and dropping Leo off. I was not happy to see him. He said morning Min. He never called me Bella, he always referred to me as Min. I asked him how his holiday had been and he said he had the best time of his life. I told him I was happy for him, but tears were rolling down my face. He asked me if I had missed him and he gave me the biggest hug and then he looked into my eyes and said, "You know Min, I will never leave you. We will be separated only through death". I felt sick to the pit of my stomach. I went to the toilet and threw up.

He asked me if I was alright and I said yes, I am fine. He couldn't help himself and made a disgusting comment "You never know you might have cancer". I couldn't believe what he said. He then further commented, "Anyway, how long do you want to live for you are getting older". I replied, "I am not old I have only just turned 50 but when are you going to stop treating me like a doormat?" He said, "If you don't like it you can leave". I saw red and yelled "You've got a nerve telling me to go. This is my home; your bags are still packed, why don't you go?" He grabbed me by the hair and gave me the hardest slap on my face, nearly knocking my teeth out. I was so angry that I scratched his face and kicked him in the nuts. I told him to get the fuck out of my house.

How many times have I asked him to leave and he always responds with the same answer? "Are you going somewhere? Do you really think you are going to find someone better than me? No, you aren't! Honey, no one wants an old boring, and foolish wench like you. Not even the nice make-up and jewellery you put on helps you. By the way, that ring you are wearing should be mine. Consider it rent as I did with our marriage. I rented you and used you for a while and now I'm returning you to yourself. No one else will have a bar of you after me. I hope you are comfortable with being alone. You will never know if you are choosing someone out of love or loneliness".

I had to go to work and once I reached I documented everything in my diary. When I came home that evening I expected him to be gone. How wrong was I? Leo went to talk to his brother that day who advised him to be nice to me because he still needed to get his green card. Leo behaved himself for a couple of weeks as he was visiting his legal appointments during the day.

Chapter Sixteen

One evening Leo forgot his mobile phone at home and I tried hard to get into it. Finally, I punched my birthdate and I was in. I went straight into the messenger and transferred all his messages to my phone. He was sending pictures of my house to his Albanian lover making her believe that it was his house. He was also telling her that anything she wanted was hers. I didn't understand as he was writing to her in Albanian. When I had the opportunity, I showed a friend of mine the messages and she taught me how to translate them on the computer. Most of the messages were him professing his undying love for her and telling her that he had purchased this beautiful house for them to live in. He forgot to mention just one small thing that the police were on his tail and he had no home let alone any respect for anyone.

My house was being watched constantly by the police as they had Leo under surveillance. They arrested him again inside one of his houses which was full of drug crops but it was Leo's own doing. Once again the lawyers got him off the charges. That same week he was asked to christen his nephew. I was not invited but Leo wanted me to go with him but I told him that I wasn't invited and that only he was invited. Leo still insisted so

I quickly got ready. I made sure I looked like a million dollars. I wore my beautiful Versace dress. I must admit it looked stunning on me. But at the party, I may as well have stayed at home because I wasn't included in any of the photos.

I tried talking to his brother's wife who was dressed from head to toe in Gucci. It wasn't bad for someone who had arrived in this country with just two pairs of undies. As we walked into the reception centre, I was asked to sit next to Leo's brother-in-law's wife, I wasn't allowed to sit with Leo. I had to sit with the women. All the women were dressed to the nines. I sat there observing them and feeling sorry for myself. All the men were sitting together and all the ladies were sitting together. Everyone spoke in their language and no one spoke to me except to say hello. I was about to leave when all of a sudden the band started playing and people started dancing. They started throwing money at the singers on the stage. I mean a lot of money, Leo himself threw at least $3,000 if not more. It seemed this was their tradition. I couldn't believe what I was seeing.

The next day one of Leo's friends and his wife came over to talk to him about some business. When the men finished talking, they went somewhere but the woman stayed and we started chatting. She told me that after the christening party Leo and his brother had gone to an Albanian club where they hang out and play cards. She also told me that she had asked her husband if I was involved in any wrongdoings and he replied that we didn't involve Bella in anything. He made sure she wasn't included in the photos or the videos so that when they were sent overseas for everyone to watch no one would question who Bella was and if they did, they would tell them that she was the babysitter. I was quite hurt by all this and when I mentioned this to Leo, he wasn't perturbed but then I didn't expect anything else from him.

Leo was often invited for dinner to his brother's house but I was never invited. Leo and his brother stuck together like glue. On one occasion all four of us drove to Melbourne. It was awful as they kept talking in Albanian and I couldn't understand a word of what they were saying. After a gruelling 8-hour drive we finally arrived. We went straight to our hotel rooms. Luckily, we had a room of our own and we immediately went off to sleep. The next morning, we all went into Charleston for breakfast and I noticed that his sister-in-law was speaking to her husband in this childish way with a baby voice. Although I didn't understand a word she was saying, I did understand that she wanted something from the Gucci store. So, after breakfast, we went to the Gucci store. I was watching her and was very happy for her as she was so excited to be receiving a Gucci handbag and Louis Vuitton shoes. I watched in awe as this woman had arrived 12 months ago in this country with an empty suitcase and today her husband and she had more money than they could spend.

As we were leaving the car park Leo almost ran over a man and his child. The boy was so scared he started crying. I said stop, stop. Leo stopped the car and got out to see if they were okay. The boy's father was upset and started yelling "What's wrong with you? Can't you see this is a pedestrian crossing?" Leo took a breath and apologized. Luckily no one was hurt. He quickly opened his wallet and gave the man a couple of hundred dollars. The man was really grateful.

We went back to our room and took an afternoon nap. We then got ready to go out for dinner. We arrived at the restaurant before Leo's brother and sister-in-law. They finally arrived and I couldn't believe how ridiculous his sister-in-law was looking. She was wearing her Louis Vuitton heels in which she could barely walk. I thought she would fall and hurt herself. Her dress was so tight that you could see every bulge of her voluptuous body. It was not a pretty sight. We had dinner and Leo took me back to the hotel room while he and his brother went out. He took all the cash we had with him. It was a substantial amount. Around 6 am Leo's sister-in-law rang me to ask if Leo was back from his night out and I responded no why? I asked her if her husband was back and she said no and that is why she was ringing me. Finally, at 8 am they returned from their night out. When I saw Leo I said, "I suppose we won't be going anywhere today?" He said you can go shopping on your own if you like. I told him I didn't have any money. I said, "You took all the money last night, can you give me some? Leo said, "No, I have spent it all." I was so angry that I caught a taxi and went for a stroll to Melbourne. I had $200 which was enough for lunch and taxi fare and perhaps enough for petrol to get me home.

Before we left for home Leo's sister-in-law wanted to take home some cakes from Brunelli's. She bought a big box full of them. We stopped a few times on the way home to have coffee and not once did she offer anyone a cake. It just went to show what type of woman she was.

A week later Leo's brother called and Leo left to go over to his place. He told me not to cook dinner for him as he didn't know when he would be home. I asked him what had happened. Leo said "My brother had gone to the market and bought some chickens and you can roast one when I return. They are fresh, ok?" Four hours later he returned with a box full of chickens. He said, "Bella, I am looking forward to this fresh roasted chicken. I turned on the oven while Leo was lying on the couch. I opened the bag to take out the chicken and when I looked inside, I asked Leo to come over and look. He asked what was wrong. I told him to come over and take a look. I said, "Where is the chicken meat? These are just chicken carcasses." Leo couldn't believe his eyes. He immediately rang his brother and started yelling at him. Leo was very angry. His brother came over to see what Leo was going on about. When he saw the bag even he couldn't believe it. Leo asked him to get out of the house.

Leo told me to get ready for dinner as he wanted to go out. That night we held hands and he apologised to me and said that no one can get away with disrespecting them. After dinner, we returned home and sat down to watch a little television. Just then there was a knock at the door and I went to see who it was. It was his brother. I opened the door and Leo was behind me. As soon as he saw his brother, he told him to get the fuck out of his house and almost pushed him down the stairs. Leo ran into the kitchen and grabbed the bag of chicken carcasses and threw them at his brother while yelling, "Never come to this house ever again". After that incident, his brother rarely came over. His wife never really spoke to me except to say hello, how are you? Nothing more. I was as it is not interested in talking to her.

She never acknowledged all that I did for her, for example, holding her hand while she gave birth to her first child. I will never forget that day. When I got to the hospital, she was already in the delivery suite with the midwife. I asked her where her husband was and she said that their religion didn't allow men to be present at the birth. I sat with her throughout the labour and finally a beautiful baby girl was born. I sent her flowers. Apparently, she didn't like them so she gave them to the nurses. When I went to visit her at home, I asked her in front of Leo why she didn't keep the flowers sent by me.

She acted all coy and innocent and said she preferred artificial flowers. I was also told to gift the child $1,000. I told Leo that there was no way I was doing this. As it is I was not very popular so why would I give a person that arrived in Australia with an empty suitcase and could hardly afford to put bread on their table and now they were acting like millionaires? I did buy the baby a beautiful dress and a little toy, but it wasn't very well received as it was not Gucci. So, I doubt the baby ever got to wear the dress gifted by me. I don't know why she always thought she was better than me. If only she knew that her husband was having affairs behind her back. He even tried to tell Leo it was okay to have affairs behind your partner's back, to mistreat your partner, and to cheat and lie.

All in the Name of Love

One night Leo's brother threw himself onto me like an animal. He was totally out of control. He threw me onto the bed and I kept yelling stop. He couldn't care less. Thank God his phone rang at that moment and he removed himself from me to answer the phone. He took the call and then quickly left the house. I was shaken up. I had a shower and tried to close my eyes and leave all my sorrows behind. I finally drifted off to sleep and awoke at 7 am the next morning. Leo was still not home. My house phone was ringing, it was Leo's brother's wife. She was looking for her husband. I said, "Sorry, I can't help you; I have no idea where they are" and I put down the phone. I had my coffee in peace and got ready for work.

The whole day I didn't hear from Leo, not that I cared. When I returned home from work, I went to open the garage door and the door wouldn't open. At first, I thought I had a flat battery. I went through the front door and walked into the garage. As I walked down the stairs into the garage I saw all the equipment for marijuana. I couldn't breathe. Leo wasn't home so I rang him and asked him to come home. When he got home, I told him to remove all his shit out of my house. He started yelling "I am the boss of this house" and I was yelling back "This is my house and you will remove all your equipment out of here now". I rang my son and told him what was going on. He quickly came over and got into an argument with Leo. He also ordered him to move all the stuff out. I told Leo he had three days.

This was the one thing I put my foot down on. Leo got angry and went upstairs. Suddenly he came downstairs holding a gun in his hands. He wanted to shoot my son but, thank God he had already left. Leo was looking for him, but he couldn't find him. I tried hard to keep my sons away from him. He was so toxic that I never once told him where they lived. What I couldn't understand was that every time we drove past a church he would do the sign of the cross three times, if he saw a black cat on the street he would turn around and go the other way as according to him it was bad luck. When we went past a cemetery, he made sure that he washed his hands or it would bring evil home.

Little did he know that he was that evil. He was one of the worst sinners. His kind has no morals or conscience, they are like leeches that just stick to you and suck your blood and get pleasure from doing so. He enjoyed making me feel small. I tried not to let him get to me, but it wasn't easy to smile through silent pain, cry behind closed doors and fight battles that no one knows about, feeling less of a person and every lesson changed me. His vicious tongue was like a poisonous snake, arrogant and rude. My loneliness was killing me. I would rather spend my days alone believing in the messy imperfect difficult vision than live with him.

One long weekend we had a beautiful night of lovemaking. Leo had such an incredible body and he knew how to charm me. The lovemaking was very intense. I knew deep down that something wasn't right. The next morning Leo said "Come on, get up, I am taking you to Victor Harbour for lunch. On the drive, his phone wouldn't stop ringing. I told him to pull over and answer the phone. He said no it was just a friend. As usual, I wasn't allowed to question him otherwise he would lose his shit. We were having a great day, we even went camel riding and jet skiing. His phone kept ringing the whole day. Leo went to the bathroom and left his phone on the table. A message popped up, "I have been ringing you all day, have you forgotten that we are going out tonight? I hope you still have a lot of energy as tonight I intend to fuck you more than once. I don't want to hear that you are tired. I can't wait to see you. Dress casual. See you at seven out front Jules xxx". So of course, we returned home at 6.30 pm. Leo made himself presentable and went off.

The same night I received a phone call from my niece and she asked "aunty Bella, is everything ok with you and Leo? I said yes of course but why are you asking? She said that she hadn't seen me for a long time and that she would be sending me a photo. So she took a photo of Leo with another woman. He was in Rundle Street. I said it was probably a friend of his and she said no aunty they are kissing and holding hands. Leo returned home at 3 am and he looked shagged. I didn't mention the other woman, I kept it to myself.

On Australia Day and Leo and I went for a drive into the hills. I just kept staring at him. I couldn't help myself from catching glimpses of his beautiful green eyes. Looking into his eyes drove me insane. When Leo looked at me with those eyes I would go into another world. I was excited to see the fireworks. We pulled up to the edge of a cliff and I looked into his green eyes once again. He was getting aroused and I started to pleasure him. He was a little rough and I couldn't breathe. I was trying to catch my breath when he grabbed me and pulled me close to him. As he pulled me towards him my knee hit the glove box. A few items spewed out of the glove box. I just ignored it. I continued pleasuring him and he climaxed at the same time as the fireworks started going off. The sky was lit up in brilliant colours. It was a beautiful sight.

As I was getting back into my seat, I felt something on the carpet and picked it up without paying too much attention. We kept watching the fireworks and once again I felt something next to my feet. I picked up a box of condoms. Five were missing from the box. I quickly got up and looked into his beautiful green eyes and said, "What are these?" Leo said, "Never mind, let's just enjoy the night and the amazing fireworks". I looked at him and said, "But what are these?" He grabbed the condoms from my hand and threw them over the cliff. I just looked at him and he looked straight into my eyes. I could not resist him anymore so I started pleasuring him again, but I just couldn't get the condoms out of my head. But Leo was now so aroused he ripped my underwear off and made love to me with the fireworks going off in the background. I was still so very sexually attracted to him. As we were driving home, I couldn't let the condoms go. I had to ask him if he was cheating on me. He replied, "What's come over you, of course not Min. A friend of mine borrowed my car and the condoms belong to him. Min, we had such a magical night don't ruin it for me". I knew Leo didn't want me to ask any questions but at the back of my mind, I knew that Leo was cheating on me. He also knew that he just had to look at me and I would melt.

When we got home, I ran a bath. Ten minutes later Leo jumped in with me. He saw that I had tears in my eyes and he wiped them away. He said, "Please tell me what's wrong?" I replied "Please do not hurt me. My heart will fix itself in time but it's my mind I need to worry about. My mind is where I lock the memories, my mind is where I have kept the pieces of the ones that hurt me in the past and that still cuts me like shards of glass. My mind keeps me up at night, makes me cry, and destroys me repeatedly. You need to convince me how those condoms got in your glove box." He responded "You know very well that every time I go out it's just with my brother. Can we please drop this?" That night Leo held me tightly in his arms. The next morning when we were having breakfast, I said something silly and he started laughing. It was such a sincere laugh and he continued smiling. I was so glad he was happy. I then started questioning my head.

I wondered what was making him smile and why couldn't I make him laugh that way before. My love for him was so strong that it didn't matter what he had done to me. Like hunger can be satisfied only to return again and again a million times stronger. It was like he had this magical power over me stealing unseen and unsuspecting of the wound of the victim sucking out life's blood. But for me, my love for him was a simple thing. It was gentle, soft, fragile, and tender as the petals of a camellia yet as strong as the roots of a willow tree. It didn't matter how strong the wind blew as it would be the last tree to stand proudly on its own. I was still madly in love with him.

The weekend was almost upon us and I was determined to catch him. I asked him on Saturday night "Are you going out tonight?" He responded, "What a stupid question, don't I go out every Saturday night and if

I feel like it every night of the week too." I told Leo I had a birthday party to attend and it wasn't far from where he was going. He said, "Ok, but ask one of your friends to drop you back home". I said, "Ok, I can do that". Leo parked the car and drove off suddenly. Then an Albanian woman who disliked him picked me up and took me for a drive. She took me to where Leo was. He was at a party with a Lebanese woman. They looked so in love, hugging and giggling. They looked very happy together.

So, with the help of this Albanian woman, I had all the power that I needed. Finally, I saw with my own eyes what a beast Leo really was. I quickly returned home and waited for him in the bedroom. When Leo finally returned home, he came straight to bed. He picked me up and demanded that I say "I love you" to him and he wanted to have sex with me. I stayed very calm telling him that I was not feeling well but that didn't deter him. He climbed on top of me like a demon on the loose and had his way with me. When he entered my vagina, I could almost feel the cum around his penis. It made me sick to my core. He was in a relationship only with himself. But inside me lived this loneliness or emptiness. I think I was half a person, the other half of me was standing at the front door of hell ready to throw him in. And I wanted to finish this nonsense. However, I had to be a whole person and not half a person as he was.

He was in this relationship only to see what he could get out of me. I had already contributed so much to this relationship. To love means to serve and to love means to go the extra mile to make the other person feel valued. Love is not about one person controlling the other but rather understanding one another. Leo didn't have any respect for women. He would use and abuse them while he cared only for his people. But for some reason he wanted everyone to love him. He thought he was God, that he was unbreakable.

It was an autumn day when I pleaded with him to leave and as usual, he laughed loudly. I didn't know how to get rid of him. Leo demanded that I change the house title to his name and then he would leave. So, I yelled, "Over my dead body, it will never happen." So as per his usual predictability, he said, "You will die sooner or later". These words became a song in my head. I had heard them so often. I felt as though I was drowning in my sorrows. At this point, I felt as if I was dying as if my tears were drowning me and I was being pulled under water. I felt as though one of these days he will choke me as I would be sitting right at the breakfast bar. I can still hear his voice loud and clear in my head. A small voice was also telling me to get up and get busy. So, I did. I felt so much better and changed my thoughts so he couldn't get into my head.

Hours later I finally decided to put an end to all of this. At that time I was noting every movement and writing down everything that was spoken by Leo. I found a fire within me. A fire I hadn't felt for a long time. It was a blazing fire causing me so much pain and at the same time, my tears were sucking me down and suffocating me. I sat on the ground and thought that the blazing fire was causing me so much pain and anxiety that I could barely breathe. Leo was suffocating me. Leo had done this to me and for what? Money? His influence and the environment around him were pure evil. He was happy and loveable one moment and the next, he would be angry and envious of others around him. None of them cared about each other. They all tried so hard to outdo one another and to see who made more money so they could brag about who had more.

One Thursday night he arrived home at about 10.30 pm with an invitation in his hand. It was an invite to his cousin's baby daughter's christening. On Saturday we went for the christening first to the church and then for brunch at the Pavilion on the Park. All of them had expensive cars. The women were dressed up to the nines where some of them looked like drag queens, way over the top. One of Leo's aunts introduced me to quite a few people. I had also made sure that I looked pretty good. Leo's aunt asked me if I was going to bear any babies with Leo. I had to be careful how I responded. I paused and then I responded, "Not now but perhaps in the future. Right now Leo isn't interested in babies he is just interested in making wealth".

Another of Leo's aunts was also at the christening. She was gossiping about me. How did I know? I could hear her conversation very clearly. She was saying that I was too old for Leo. She didn't care that I could hear what she was saying. She also asked me where I had bought my degree. By then I was getting a little angry. As Leo was busy mingling around I was left alone. I connected with another Italian Australian woman sitting opposite me at the table and started whispering to her with my serviette in front of my mouth so others couldn't lip-read what I was saying. I said, "This is who I am, this is what I don't want to be. It will be one cold day in hell before I start behaving like them". She told me to be very careful and trust very little. As I listened to her the words cut me deep.

Seeing all that falseness I couldn't walk away easily as I was stuck on Leo. He came back to the table to show everyone that he was the perfect partner. But little did they know that behind closed doors he was a different person. He said to me "Please remember me for the good times and the magic that we shared. You see Min I need to grow up. You are the most beautiful woman here". Words such as these would lure me back in, they were like quicksand. Maybe I overreacted. I was constantly in situations where I was totally frustrated. But I couldn't say anything because I knew the consequences. I didn't dare challenge him.

Leo said all this to me with a smile so everyone could see how happy we were. I whispered to myself, "Screw what everybody thinks." I felt completely abandoned and was afraid to love because they would leave me. I thought there wasn't any future for us. I was so frustrated and he was obsessed with shocking people and believed that his way was the right way. He was so desperate to prove himself to everyone even if it meant doing illegal dealings. They were under-skilled, desperate, misunderstood stupid human beings that I had ever come across in my life. My actions or my words meant very little to any of them. But I lived the life that he had chosen for himself. I wasn't happy with Leo's criminal associations and I was desperate to put my foot down no matter what. I wasn't going to jeopardise my career for him. Living life in an impulsive way was not for me.

I needed to face the consequences of my actions and my words. They were strong words but there was no turning back and from that moment on I took control of my destiny and proved to everyone who was trying to hold me down or make me afraid that no matter what, no one could take my soul. At the end of the day, it was that authentic truth inside me which kept me going and helped me to rise. Everyone is a master of their destiny. I have to decide my destiny for myself. Helping people daily in my line of work reminded me that my job was not yet done and it helped others to become better versions of themselves, and this was my calling in life. But his only motive was to kill me and get my money.

One day I learned that Leo's visa had expired. In the morning he had to meet with the immigration officials. The lawyers told him that things didn't look good for him, so the night before he took all his gold, the boat, and all his valuable possessions to his evil brother's house. Both of them were using me in a very manipulative way. I kept receiving all the invoices from the lawyers. I rang his evil brother and he and the lawyer applied for a special visa for Leo which cost another $7,000. My funds were running dry. I wanted to meet Leo's brother, but he refused. I went to see the immigration lawyers and they organised for me to speak about Leo saying that he deserved to stay in Australia. I did as I was told as I was addicted to Leo like a drug addict is addicted to drugs. I begged his lawyers to help him.

Not once did his brother and his wife pick up the phone to enquire about his well-being. There was not a single phone call from them. I felt as though I was being controlled by both brothers. So, I decided to take matters into my own hands. I took a day off from work to put an end to all this madness. I went to see Leo's lawyer. I handed him $5,000 to pay for the visa but I didn't pay for the one his brother had ordered for $7,000. I also made it very clear to the lawyer that from that day onwards he was not to send any more invoices to my home as I would no longer be contributing any money toward his fees. And I asked him to lose my address.

I told Leo, "You have been using me and abusing my generosity for far too long. Your people's opinions and judgements put me in darkness. The past is now behind me. Whatever happened whether the unjust, cruel, harsh, or whatever the case may be, I was never any good no matter what I did." Leo pleaded with me to go and ask my ex-husband for a loan and I said, "How will you repay him? Why don't you ask one of your girlfriends to help you or your gangster brother?" Not once did anyone ask how I was, my heart was pounding. I knew in my heart that he didn't care about me, and I kept telling myself "you are just being used, don't allow yourself to be controlled by anyone, let go and move on and don't allow him to control the direction of my life." My fear was judgement and others people's opinions. But at that moment I knew in my heart that Leo would never miss me, he could have said anything but I no longer cared. I remembered all the times he had pushed me and then bribed his way back into my life. How poorly I had been treated by his sick twisted mind or how my face had become his punching bag every time I said no to his demands. Now I want to see how he would bribe his way back to his country.

Chapter Seventeen

There came a point in my life where I realized who mattered, I learnt which people surrounding me were fake, who was true, and who would risk their all for me if they ever got caught by Leo or members of his family. I knew what they were capable of. I had learnt the biggest lesson of my life. God, who saw me through all this, never hated me, never told my business to anyone unless I trusted them completely. God also gave generously to live a simple life and forgave quickly. I remember all the lessons that I had learnt, all my cuts and bruises. They are stored in the deep consciousness of my mind. I imagined getting a needle and sewing up my mouth. When I get back my power and I will pick up a pair of scissors and slowly, slowly start cutting the stitches and my voice will be heard. Hopefully, I would learn to be kind always and remember that God works in mysterious ways. Sometimes I felt that God was not on my side, I felt the power of the devil that wanted my soul, but I didn't let it happen. The darkness made me see the light.

One evening after Leo had beaten me badly, he left me to go and see another woman. An Asian girlfriend. I picked up a pair of scissors and started a conversation

All in the Name of Love

with the devil. I remember it so vividly; My eyes were closed and I was pointing the scissors at his forehead. I was yelling at him "You are not going to fucking kill me you son of a bitch. Just watch me, wait, and see what I will do to you with the help of the Albanian woman. She wouldn't hesitate in helping me because of all the generosity I have given her. I won't have to lift a finger. If she is caught by the police she has all the information with an envelope full of hair and all the photos of my beaten-up face and body. She would tell the police that she was in danger. She would get home detention for a month and as for him, his days are numbered."

A couple of nights before he got arrested he had come over and begged me for $30,000 because he was in debt. I told him the answer was no, "Sorry I can't help you anymore." I refused to let Leo in that night. We were standing at the front door with the light on. We both noticed a police car driving by very slowly on my street. He begged me to let him in the house. I said, "No, this is my house it will never be yours." I was holding my phone very tightly and told him if he didn't leave, I would ring the police. He requested me to lend him the money since he was in trouble. He said he knew I had the money. I said, "I used to have money, but you and your family are like leeches and you have sucked me dry. I have nothing left to give. So, please leave." He finally decided to leave and started walking down the stairs.

He told me about his girlfriend in Albania and that I would be sorry and that he was the best thing that had ever happened to me. I yelled, "Fuck you, good riddance to bad rubbish." His English was so bad that he wheeled the rubbish bin out onto the curb. I said to myself, "What the hell is wrong with this idiot?" I was so angry that as he left I locked all the doors and ran to my next-door neighbour to tell them that Leo no longer lived with me and if they saw him around not to talk to him but to just call the police. A few days later the Albanian woman told me that he had got arrested and had been deported back to Albania. I immediately blocked him from all my social media and slowly started rebuilding my life.

I chose to love him in silence because there is no rejection in silence; I chose to love him in loneliness for in loneliness no one owns you but me. I chose to let him go because his greediness didn't deserve someone as genuine as me and distance shielded me from all the pain that he had inflicted. I chose to hold him always in my prayers and hoped that God was merciful on his soul, and I chose to hold him in my dreams for he had no end in my dreams. But I am writing a letter to the universe wherein I'll specify all the horror that you had brought into my life. Then I will burn the letter and release the ashes into the wind for the wind is gentle and it will take him away into the universe so they can deal with someone like him.

Truth is everything and I won't give up. He is not worthy of giving up anything for. Everything that he did will hurt for a while but he is not even worth suffering for. I would like to promise myself that I would never let anyone get comfortable disrespecting me. Disagreements will happen but when someone undermines me, they are not worthy of my time. Most importantly, he taught me not to put up with disrespect. I don't need that shit,

I will fuck them off and every time he broke me I will mend. He thought that I was dead and that he could bury me, but I rose.

TO LEO: Throw everything you have at my heart and watch me do more than just survive. You will see all the storms, all the things you have done to me, they will come and get you by surprise. Just like you got me by surprise, plenty more surprises will be in store for you, just wait and see. Just wait for the sunrises. As for Leo's older brother, he was the evillest, the worst demon that could exist in hell. He is the worst burnt piece of wood in hell. His soul is black to the core and everything around him is fake. Just like his soul and the name given to him Leca, matches his evil personality. He is the one who hides behind the door in the dark, holding a sharp knife, and sticks it in your back and you don't know where it came from. He was evil to the core with no education whatsoever but very streetwise. He crawls up anyone's arse if he knows he can gain something from them. He is so greedy and hungry for money that I am sure that he has sold his soul to the devil and his two other brothers are the two puppets that he dangles on a string. When he landed in Australia, he had nothing. He put a lot of pressure on my partner demanding $1,000 a week. Back then $1,000 was a lot of money. They were out and about every night of the week introducing him to all the members of the Albanian gangsters, which he started welcoming into my house. Every time I asked who these people were, I was told they are friends.

One particular night I had a few friends over and he had a few of his friends over as well. I remember clearly that in the morning Leo asked me to change the bed.

I didn't argue with him I just changed the bed as he requested. He also asked me to change the ensuite towels with the Versace towels. I thought to myself "What the hell?" Around 7 pm my guests arrived. Half an hour later so did a member of his family. He was very charming to one of my friends. I noticed Leo nudge him and they went upstairs. Five minutes later they came back downstairs. Half an hour later I noticed my girlfriend and his friend going upstairs. I asked Leo why they were going upstairs. The evil brother replied "He probably wants to show her the balcony," so I said okay. I heard my bedroom door slam. I went halfway up the stairs, but his evil brother stopped me. He said, "Let them be. They are just having a bit of fun." He added, "Why do you care about her? She's been married three times. She knows what she is doing."

Meanwhile, Leca had had a few drinks and he started telling us how he had been living in Italy and pushing cocaine and he also had a few prostitutes working for him. He had been caught by the police and he was in serious trouble. Apparently, a particular police officer had it in for him. This officer had bashed one of his working girls. He also commented that a woman should not be heard. That did not sit well with me. I had to open my mouth and I replied "A woman has as many rights as any man. Females are equivalent to males. No one has the right to hit a woman". I looked at his wife and said, "Do you understand what I just said?" She didn't respond, she didn't say anything, she quickly looked down at her feet.

Of course, her evil husband was talking about how he had lived in Italy for many years and then he had gone to Albania where he first laid eyes on his wife in a church. She was with her mother. He had no idea who she was, but he asked some of the older ladies and they told him which family she belonged to and one month later they were married. It didn't take long for him to start putting his wife down in front of all of us, "You are nothing, you are overweight, you have big ears and you are also uneducated." His wife was too scared to answer him back, so I felt the need to step in, "If you don't care for her why in god's name did you marry her?" He responded, "To give me a son and to cook and clean". His wife bore him a beautiful daughter. But he was not happy with the newborn daughter as he desperately wanted a son.

I replied, "Your daughter is beautiful, but I guess beauty is nothing if your tongue is ugly." I couldn't believe how upset he was just because he didn't have a baby boy. He was drinking himself stupid. He forgot that the only reason he got his wife pregnant was so he could stay in Australia. He also had the best immigration lawyers that money could buy. Both of them had arrived in Australia with fake passports telling the lawyers that he was a refugee in their country and on top of that the Red Cross was supporting them with money. He had plenty of money through his drug dealings and his lies. I was asked to leave and it suited me just fine. I couldn't stand being around such men. He drank too much, smoked too much, spent money recklessly, laughed too little, and drove too fast.

One day he was picked up for speeding and wanted me to use my points so he wouldn't lose his license. He was forever making demands. He got very angry, stayed up late, and woke up tired all the time. He put Leo through a lot of stress looking after all the crops. One night I went to visit his newborn child and asked his wife, "How are you coping with being a mum?" He turned towards her with rage in his eyes and said, "I don't want her touching the baby". He was referring to me. Once again, I couldn't hold back and responded, "If you hate me, hate me alone, don't be out there lying about me and trying to recruit people to hate me. I don't think you realise how much I have sacrificed for your family. You keep telling me Leo is too young. What's your excuse? You are constantly looking for problems while I have been nothing but loyal to you". I started walking away and noticed his wife was throwing food in the bin. I said, "Why are you throwing all this good food?" She said, "It has been in the fridge for over a week". Why were these people so ungrateful for what they had?

I was silently getting angry and sometimes the best advice to take was my own. Preventing their behaviour from destroying my heart. I never apologized for what I said as it felt like saying sorry for being there and most of all for being real. It took me a long time to understand who the monsters were. How someone like me could even think about it? I was getting angry about the wastage of food. So many people in this world had no food at all and so I was frustrated and I had to speak out. It was difficult to forgive someone who chose to hurt me. But after a lot of soul searching, I realized that forgiveness was not about accepting or excusing their behaviour, it was about letting go so the beast is unable to own our soul. So, as I said, sometimes the best advice is your own, preventing their behaviour from destroying your heart. I never apologized for what I felt. My heart cried out for help and every night I would ask the higher powers for help. As God knows I felt abandoned, numb to any emotions because I was a slave and my bitter pill was when I stopped searching for acceptance or rejection. But I must admit that my belief pulled me out of a very dark place, and I wouldn't wish such a situation even upon my worst enemy.

It was during the worst storms of my life that I saw the true colours of those beasts who once made me believe that they cared for me. So, I took their opinion with a grain of salt. In the end, it's not what they thought of me it's what I thought about myself that counted. I had to do what was best for me and to succeed I had to first improve to improve. I had to first practice to practice. I had to first learn to walk in the footsteps of the devil. I had to first learn that I could not afford to fall and that I had to dance to the beat of his drum.

I could not believe in myself though I know that there was something inside me that was greater than any obstacle. At that point, I really didn't care and I didn't care if any of those demons liked me or disliked me. I wasn't put on this earth to entertain anyone. If anyone wanted to love me for my money they would never succeed. I never forgot and I would always be 10 steps ahead of my enemies. I have faced more in my life than most people can ever imagine but it's up to me to tell the difference between the genuine and the fake people in my life. I don't have to waste time on people who weren't worth it. The truth is to become me; the truth is that it won't be easy, but I reached the other side and realised that all along there had been a reason, a plan, and it was that my home was their destination.

One day Leo was in the garage when he yelled for me to come as he needed help with something. I went to the garage and found that he was looking for some of his drug money. He had hidden it and couldn't find it. Every time he started raising his voice my panic attacks started getting worse. He asked me to help him to look for the money. I said, "I don't believe that you don't know where you put the money." He punched me in the face. Just like that. I sat on the ground crying, talking to myself and calling out for help from Archangel Michael. I asked him for help. I had been through so much in my life, the pain, the struggle, and the hardships. Things I never thought I would be able to ever get through. But I had and I always would but at that point in time, I prayed for him to help me. "I am in a very bad relationship. I need your help, please watch over me, I can't do this on my own anymore. Are you watching this? I am very angry and I need you to help me." Suddenly, I heard his voice loud and clear, "Keep your chin up, keep moving forward, and keep shining. The pain, struggles and hardships are almost over". He kept talking, "I am going to take you for a walk, hold my hand and come with me." I wasn't scared of dying.

I took his hand and he took me below to a dungeon. There were all sorts of people there, elderly, children and middle aged. All those people had chains on their feet. They were also very dirty. I started getting a little scared when an angel appeared and I started rebelling. I said, "I don't belong here, I wasn't a bad person". So, he said, "Okay, let me see what I can do. He looked above and a face appeared in the sky. He said, "Turn around" and there was a beautiful crystal-clear river. I immediately recognised the river. It was where I used to jump on the rocks free as a bird with no worries in the world. The voice from above said, "If you can jump those three slippery rocks without falling into the water you can stay here, you won't have to go home anymore, but if you fall you can't stay." I said to myself, "This is a piece of cake". I got myself into position and jumped onto the first rock, it wasn't easy but I landed on the rock with both feet. I was petrified because it was very slippery.

I took a deep breath and jumped safely onto the second rock. As I looked down into the water, I saw a huge snake circling. My legs started trembling. I needed to jump onto the last rock. So once again I took a deep breath and jumped. One foot landed on the rock. It was so slippery that my foot slipped into the water. I was sitting there in the dark and again I heard the voice from above, "Run, run as fast as you can otherwise the snake will see you". As I got up, I heard Leo's voice, "Bella, I've found the money". I asked, "What do you mean?" He replied, "I had left it at a friend's place." I was confused and thought what the hell was this all about? I decided that I wasn't going to cry, I was going to shine. From that day on I decided to let him go to the dungeon of hell. That night I felt that I had died but it seems my job on earth had not yet finished. I had to right some wrongs. I had to fix all the bad karma that I had inflicted on myself. I had to get Leo out of my life. It wasn't going to be easy but I had to find the strength to get him out. Justice had to be served.

I knew that every time he said "I love you" some bad would come to me sooner or later. They would love me only as much as they could use my loyalty and that's where the benefits stop. My eyes would see him, but my soul felt the pain. The fearful words that came out of his mouth were very damaging. At times, the words were deadly when he looked at me with those evil eyes. It was like I was his addiction. His heart was made of liquid sunsets. There was nothing I wouldn't do to make him pay. I can't tolerate fake people and liars. I prefer to walk alone than be surrounded by insincere people. I noticed every movement in detail and all the strange people who came into my home. They took advantage of my kindness. If I could kill them with the Holy water to hell fire I would gladly do so. Leo treated me worse than a dog with chains on my feet and no way out from those evil horrible brothers. They were in charge of my perfect heaven and I was locked in the dungeon of hell.

That was no random meeting. I believe there are no random meetings in our lives. Everyone we touch and who touches us is sent for a reason. He had to cross my path for a reason. Even the briefest encounter could open a door or heal a wound or close a circle that had been started long before our birth. Finally, I am still alive to tell my story. I was back with the key to the throne in my hands and in this life no one could ever convince me to hand over the key. A lesson had been well learnt and from that day on when I looked back at the past, I could smile and say to myself, "I never thought I could do it, but I did. I overcame all the people who tried to take everything that belonged to me and tried to bring me down to my knees. I had an enormous amount of mental and emotional baggage. It had cluttered my mind. I needed to learn how to select my thoughts in the same manner as I select my clothes every day. Thank God I am alive. They tried everything in their power to control me, but in many cases, life works on controlling our minds.

Ultimately, the only things he controlled were his secrets and lies. It killed our relationship. No matter how careful one is you will get caught. What is done in the darkness always comes to light. Most of the time I played the role of a fool, the fool who thinks they are fooling you. I balanced myself on the thread of my thoughts and hoped not to fall. Looking out for myself wasn't easy. He had big dreams for himself and his family. His mind was full of dreams and manufactured illusions. Illusions are the beast of all pleasures but his illusions were not reality.

Chapter Eighteen

A couple of months later it was my birthday and I asked Leo what we would be doing to celebrate. He said that all his family would be going out for dinner. He was out most of the day and told me to be ready by 7 pm as we would be going for dinner and dancing. I waited till 7.30 pm and then finally called him asking how long he would be. He told me that sorry, there have been a change in the plans as his family and he had been invited to a friend's for a BBQ and that we would celebrate another time. I was so upset I called my friend. She came over and also brought a bottle of Moet for my birthday. After she left, I went to bed and cried myself to sleep.

The next morning, I got up and went off to work as if nothing had happened. My job of solving other people's problems kept my mind away from what was happening in my life. I was recognized in my field of work and there was also an article about me in the newspaper. Leo was very proud of my achievement and took me to a casino to celebrate. There was a live band playing in another area of the casino and during the night he kept going there without me. I felt he was meeting with someone else. Finally, we came home and he made love to me.

All in the Name of Love

The next day he told me that we had been invited to a wedding but he never told me the date. He just said that I should make sure that I look immaculate. I went out and bought a very expensive designer-label dress. He loved the dress. One night he got dressed in a very smart suit and told me he was going for dinner with his friends. A few hours later, one of my family members rang me and asked if I had broken up with Leo. Apparently, he was at the same wedding as her with another woman and they seemed very close. I replied it couldn't be him as he had gone out with his friends for dinner and that she must have made a mistake. But she hadn't as she took a video of the happy couple and sent it to me. Sure enough, it was him at the wedding he was supposed to take me to. I was heartbroken. I transferred the video to another phone that he didn't know about and did not mention anything to him when he came home. He thought I was asleep, but I was only pretending. I waited till he fell asleep and was snoring and then tried to get into his phone, but he had changed the password. I worked out his password and got into his photos. He even had photos with her parents and they seemed like a very happy couple. I carefully sent them to my secret phone and deleted all evidence. This caused me a lot of stress, so I decided to take a week off work as it was affecting my job. He continued as if everything was normal.

During the week off I kept a close eye on him and noticed that every morning at 10 am he would get a message. One morning he was still fast asleep at 10 am when the message came through on his phone. I quickly wrote down the number and rang it from my secret phone.

A girl answered and I asked her why she was messaging my partner. Her reply was "Who is your partner?" I said his name is Leo, but she said she didn't know anyone by that name. I responded with how funny that he gets a message at 10 am every day from your phone. But she was adamant that she did not know any Leo. She hung up on me, but within five minutes she began calling Leo's phone. Luckily his phone was on silent, so I grabbed it and went out to the balcony to answer it. Of course, it was the same girl who told me she didn't know him. She asked me who I was and I told her that I was his partner. He had used the same line on her as with the first woman that he is with an old lady for the sake of getting citizenship.

She asked me if I was in the bedroom with him, but I told her that I was on the balcony. She then told me that they were getting married and he had already met her parents. I told her, "I don't mind him marrying you, but can you ask him to move in with you so you can support him as I have done it for long enough." She asked me "How can you support him when he is rich and has a building in the city?" Since this was not true I asked her who had given him a building and money because when he had moved in, he only had a garbage bag full of dirty clothes. I confronted Leo with this information and he admitted that they were friends and that's all. So, I made him call her in front of me and break it off.

He rang her and suddenly looked like he had seen a ghost. The blood drained from his face. He hung up and had to sit down. I asked him if he was ok. He said, "You know Bella, the wedding that I went to six months ago, where you were supposed to come with me and I went alone?" I replied, "Stop with your lies. While I was at home you were playing lovers with someone else. Anyways what happened?" He replied, "Well, the groom got murdered." I asked innocently "Would you like to talk about it?" To my surprise, Leo proceeded to tell me that this man had been driving home on his own from the city in the early hours of the morning and someone followed him home. A passer-by walking his dog found him on his front lawn. He had been cut open with a machete and his guts had spilled out. I was lost for words; I didn't know what to say to him. I just stood there frozen. I had a big pain in my heart and Leo started crying. He asked me if he could hug me. I also started crying as I could see his shock and pain. I couldn't bear to see him in so much pain. I realised that I was still madly in love with him, but I also had so much hatred towards him. I had to find the strength to open the wounds, stick my hands inside and pull out the core of the pain that was holding my memories and make peace with them for all that they had done to me. Although Leo and I weren't married, he had made so many promises but unfortunately, he couldn't keep even one.

Leo attended the funeral with his lover and her parents. I was just starting to again forgive him and trust him a little. When I am unforgiving and carry animosity, he feeds the very soul of conflict that keeps my pain alive.

It wasn't too long before he was at it again. This time it was with two different women. One he flew over from America and the other was a woman who provided him with houses so he could carry on doing his illegal business. This woman's name was Star and at the time all this happened, I was working as a psychologist. I had a young female client who was struggling with the passing of her father. She came to see me on several occasions. She wasn't coping very well as she had kept many secrets from her father and he passed before she had the chance to own up to what she had done. Slowly she started picking up and seemed happier. One day I said to her that she looked like a woman in love. She smiled and said that she had just met someone and that he treated her well... amazing was the word she used.

She told me how sweet he was and how he spoilt her. He was as generous as he was wealthy. During one of our conversations, I said to her that if you learn to forgive everything can change. She told me that they had no secrets between them and that he was married, but it wasn't a real marriage as he was with her only to get his papers and anyway she was old. I replied to her that it only takes two seconds to hurt someone but a long time to recover. At that point, I felt sick to my stomach because this could only be my husband since it was the same story I had heard so often before. I asked if she had a photo and I was shocked when she showed me.

I closed my eyes and tears started flowing down my face. I said to her, "Your wings are ready to fly but my heart is not ready to get broken all over again. You are looking at the old lady." I looked straight into her eyes and said, "Don't confuse my personality with my attitude. My personality is who I am, but my attitude depends on who you are. That is my husband but I'm not here to ruin your happiness or tell you what to do as you are a grown-up woman and you should do as you please."

But I was devastated and even with everything that he had done to me I still loved him, and I had convinced myself that everything would work out in the end. When I got home, he was not there so I sat on my staircase and waited till he got home around 11.30 pm. I was anxious as I thought he would be angry and I would cop it that night. To my surprise, he said nothing, walked past me, and said good night. I didn't understand what was happening, so I closed my eyes, took a deep breath, and prayed to God, "I know this is your plan, but you have to help me through it." I went to bed still in fear for my life, thinking he would suffocate me with a pillow while I was sleeping.

The next morning, I got up, made coffee when he came downstairs, sat at the breakfast bar, and asked, "Bella, why do you cry?" I replied, "I cry not because I am weak, I cry because I have been strong for too long." I grabbed my bag and left for work. As I was walking out the door, I turned to him and said "I feel sorry for you" and left. The next day she wanted to see me again, so she turned up at my office. I asked her why she had come as she had seen me just the day before. She replied, "We need to talk about Leo. I can't believe that you are the old lady he talks about. You are so beautiful, but he makes you out to be a 70-year-old wrinkly old lady." I showed her pictures of him with me out at dinner, at bars and nightclubs. She was devasted and decided that she would take revenge.

I asked her how she had met Leo. "At a bar" she replied where he had approached her and offered to buy her a drink. They had chatted for a while and then Leo asked her if she had a boyfriend to which she replied yes.

He then went on to ask if she was looking for a new one as he found her very attractive. She said, "No thank you. I already have one." But she was very attracted to him and found him charming. Leo then insisted on going home with her but she again refused. He then suggested that she cheat on her boyfriend and Leo would give her everything she wanted as he was a wealthy businessman. She asked him how such a good-looking successful businessman did not have a partner, to which he had replied, I do not have much luck with women, so please, please he pleaded be with me. She then asked that he must be having girlfriends. He replied that he had a girlfriend but she got married and she didn't want to continue with him so she ended it. After a few dates, she decided to tell him the truth as she really did not have a boyfriend and she was starting to have strong feelings for him, plus he was amazing in bed. He too decided to tell the truth that he was in a relationship with an old lady purely to get permanent residency in Australia. And that she meant nothing to him and he was only using her.

A week later he told me he was going on a business trip. I was on Facebook and I saw that he had checked into Hotel Versace with an Albanian/American woman, who sang at private Albanian functions. They spent two weeks there, while I was home on my own and working. He gave her a good time and no expense was spared on her, but he never rang me even once to see how I was, just to ask for money so he could act like a millionaire. When he came back, he acted as if nothing had happened because he thought I believed he was away on a business trip with his brother, but I knew everything.

After he returned, he was constantly on the phone messaging but he would say he was checking his Facebook account. Actually, he was sending videos of my house to this woman, pretending that it was his. She said that it was a beautiful house, but could he please put in a swimming pool as well? I confronted him again about this and he told me he wanted to marry this woman and I told him that to do so he would have to move out, to which he responded, "I am never leaving this house. How long do you want to live because you are going to die?" I felt as if he was planning to kill me and I was always looking over my shoulder for something to happen. I learned a very hard lesson, not to expect anything from people because today you are everything and tomorrow you are no one. There is always a reason why we need people, so I decided to better myself. I had two choices - either to live or just die. I was not going to allow this monster to destroy me.

Chapter Nineteen

In this world, some narcissists believe in their masks, no matter how many people they hurt along the way. They find a way to justify every horrible thing they do. What baffles me is that they genuinely believe they are good people.

Despite my human existence and my suffering I am divine, I have fallen and yet I have dared to stand up again. I've been wounded and yet had the courage to love again. The proof is that I am still standing today, but it took great inner strength.

Are we ever free or is there always someone or something which stops us from being free? But do we cry for help? And even if we do, does anyone listen? Sometimes we think that freedom is good for us just like a child in a candy store who wants everything but sometimes freedom can be very lonely. Do we really have the courage to be free? Sometimes we have to pay the price. I have never felt free. I have always had to answer to someone. As a child, I had to answer to my parents, when I got married at I had to answer to my husband and his family and now I must answer to Leo. When the hell is it my turn? As much as I have loved these two men in my long-term relationships, I have always felt trapped with no way out. When I have had to answer Leo I have felt as if I am fighting a war. He used to call me Gypsy.

One day Leo was calling me, "Come here, Gypsy". I went straight up to him and on his face, I said, "If I am a Gypsy why don't you get one of your Albanian people to help your friend? Why hassle me? This is the last thing I need in my life. By the way, my name is Bella, not Gypsy! This Gypsy is going to put a spell on you. I promise you that when you think you are flying high, I will pluck all your feathers and snap both your wings. You will then be that bye-bye blackbird who killed himself while he was trying to fly." When I finished saying all that he had no idea what I had said. Instead, he turned around and said, "I am hungry, go and make me something to eat." I made him bacon and eggs on toast. I sat on the breakfast bar watching him eat. He ate with such gusto like he hadn't eaten for days.

Watching him I said, "Slow down or you will choke yourself". In my heart I was thinking, please choke! But at that time I would have done whatever he asked and actually, I did. He asked me to drop some stuff off at one of his friends on the way home from work. I took the bags not knowing what was in them. I had a quick look when I was putting them in the boot of my Mercedes Benz. They were full of marijuana. Throughout the way, I was panicking. I kept telling myself to stay calm. Suddenly the police pulled me over. I was so scared, but the police just wanted me to do a breath test. They asked me if I had been drinking and I told them that no, I am a psychologist and am running late for work.

The policeman was very kind and let me go. Thank God, someone above was watching over me.

When I got home from work that evening, I was seething. I told Leo what had happened with the police. He responded with "Oh God you had over 30 pounds of marijuana in the boot. You would have gone to jail for a very long time". I looked at him with anger and said, "How the hell can you do that to me? What the hell is wrong with you?" He came towards me, grabbed me, and put me on the breakfast bar. He started hugging and kissing me saying "You are gorgeous. I am going to buy you everything that your heart desires". After some time, Leo went for a shower as he had to go and see someone at around 7 o'clock.

I was in bed and heard Leo returning home at around 11 o'clock. He was bragging that he had over $80,000 in cash in his bag. He came into the bedroom and emptied the money onto the bed and started counting it. I asked him where had he gotten all the money and he replied, "From your delivery today". I replied, "This is too much for me" but he knew how to butter me up. We made passionate love and of course, everything was rosy once again and I bowed to his majesty one more time.

Once again, he brought a friend of his and asked me to help him. How could I refuse the love of my life? I was so blinded. There were moments when he made me feel so empty and angry and estranged. There were many moments of sadness and emptiness.

On August 23rd, Leo went out to meet a woman on her birthday. It had been arranged by his evil brother.

He had gone for coffee during the day and he returned at 6 pm. I asked him what he wanted for dinner. But he said, "Sorry I forgot to mention but I have to go to a friend's birthday tonight. I will be home late, ok?" He went to the birthday party but he returned home early. It was very unusual but I didn't say anything.

In the morning at approximately 10.30 am there was a knock at my door. A woman with very short hair stood there. She was dressed in a very masculine way. She introduced herself as Milly, Leo's business partner. She said, "He asked me to meet him here." Very politely I invited her in and asked her to wait. I quickly ran up the stairs to wake up Leo. I came back downstairs and offered Milly a cup of coffee as I already had a pot on the breakfast bar. She accepted and we started chatting. I explained to her that Leo had gone out the previous night so was still sleeping. She responded, "Yes it was my birthday. Would you like to see some photos?" I said yes of course. I looked at the photos and sure enough there he was, the evil brother. He was all over Milly in the photos. I noticed that she had kept all the locations of all the places they had hung out at. I said to myself, "You are just what I needed".

From then on I started treating her like a queen. I needed to gain her trust. But at the same time, I was extremely cautious. Before you knew it, she was confiding in me and I was very professional with her and helped her in every possible way. I even offered her one of my properties for very little rent. She made excuses as to why she couldn't pay rent as she had to help her family since they had nothing to eat. I never pressed the matter as I wanted her to trust me.

One day Milly booked an appointment to see me, but she used a bogus name. I was very surprised when she walked into my office. She looked very stressed. I promised her that whatever she said in my office would remain in the office. I realised that she puts up a tough exterior but she was a very broken person. She was embarrassed about what had happened the previous night. I calmed her. She was very restless and then she started telling me what had taken place. Milly was in her room and around midnight she received a call from Leo's evil brother. He wanted to talk business. She let him into her room but deep down she knew he didn't want to talk business. He pushed her onto the bed and climbed on top of her like a demon on the loose. He put one hand over her mouth and raped her brutally.

I advised her to report this to the police. I told her "He has raped you and it is a very serious offence. You can't let him get away with it." Milly was frightened and said, "I can't. If I report him they will kill my family back home". I convinced her to at least see a doctor, so I made an appointment for her. I also advised her that under no circumstances was she to open the door to him again.

Milly told me that she had confided in someone else that she knew, but he must have said something to the evil brother because he went straight to her room and caught her by surprise. Once again, he forced himself into Milly's room and put a knife to her throat promising that the next time she said anything to anyone she was as good as dead. I showed her how to use her phone and to press location when she was with them, just in case he carried out his threat.

All in the Name of Love

After this Milly started trusting me and confiding in me. She told me all about Leo including the password to his telephone. She showed me photos of Leo with different girls. I had her on my side and got all the information I needed to get this beast out of my life. He had even sent Milly a photo of him and the Albanian singer with his tongue down her throat. He was despicable. I felt sick to my stomach and to this day it makes me sick when I think about it.

I always remained cautious around Milly as I didn't trust her for even a second. Every time I saw her, I had to hide my feelings of a shattered heart behind a fake smile. I knew what I had to do. I had to be patient and learn to wait because sometimes patience receives the best reward and shady people betray our trust. One should allow them in but should never sink to their level. Their choices are a direct reflection of who they are. No matter how angry, hurt, or disappointed I was I never allowed them to make me bitter. I just knew that I wouldn't let them get away with it. Though my heart was torn and like a storm, the worst was yet to come. Love does not exist in this culture nor can it be hidden where it truly does exist.

I like to look elegant, and I like to be loved and I guess when Leo saw me dressed elegantly, he also saw dollar signs and I became his victim. I should have seen the red flags instead my life with them was torture and misery. It was a painful experience. I stumbled and fell but I never let anything stop me from getting back up. I need to trust only those who can see the sorrow behind my smile, the love behind my anger, and the reason behind my silence. In the end all that remains are my actions.

I have left behind the memories and how they made me feel. Whatever I have left is to be remembered with love. No matter how hard I tried I was never good enough for them.

One afternoon I came home from work and made myself a cup of coffee. I took my high heels off and sat at the breakfast bar. Just then Leo returned home. He had been running around with Milly pushing his drugs. Leo said that I must cook as he was having a few boys over that night. I replied, "No, I am not cooking; I have told you loud and clear that you are not doing business from here. Do you understand you are not dragging me down with you"? He said, "Fine!" Suddenly Milly said, "Don't speak to my brother like that". I raised my voice and said "Since when has Leo become your brother? He is my partner, not yours. How dare you come into my home and use that tone of voice with me. This is my home and I demand a little woman-to-woman respect. While you are running around with my man, I walked alone. I walk these empty streets where my shadow is the only one that keeps me company and the only one that walks beside me. I don't need you so don't you dare speak down to me in my own home. Do you understand?" She was lost for words and became quiet.

I continued speaking, "If you think for one minute that you are going to treat me like them then you are mistaken. This is my home and I walk alone with my shadows, the only one that walks with me, as I don't remember any of you walking by my side. I understand that you are looking for other people to make you feel complete. Leo told me all about you, everyone has untold stories of pain and sadness which is life, so stop

All in the Name of Love

judging. Instead try to understand what you guys put me through because in the end if something happens to me, none of you will give a damn." I turned to Leo and said, "If you want someone to cook, show this dog how to cook because I am not cooking for anyone." Leo spoke for the first time, "Please do it just this once, do it for your gorgeous" he came over and gave me a hug and a kiss. How could I say no to that face but I felt humiliated. I said to her, "Can I please have a moment with Leo?"

She went outside and that moment felt like an eternity. I said to Leo, "Be careful with that woman. She can't be trusted." He replied, "I have everything under control. If she ever double-crosses me my family back home will kill her family." I quickly shut up. I rang and organised with the restaurant down the road to cater and deliver the food and they served up plenty of food. I excused myself and went up to the master bedroom to watch TV. But they were making so much noise downstairs that I just couldn't sleep. Leo finally came to bed in the early hours of the morning. He had a bag full of money. There was an excess of $90,000 in cash. He asked me to help him count. He then said, "I have to send this money to my village back home to build a house". While we were counting the money, Leo didn't even offer $5 to me. He was all about his brother, his family, and his people.

The following Saturday Leo was out all day. He rang me at 4:30 pm and told me "Get ready, we are going out for dinner". I was ready by 6 pm. Leo arrived home with Milly. I was ready and waiting. I had decided to wear a long dress. She said "You look beautiful" and

I thanked her for the compliment. She looked at me and said "I wish I could look like that." Leo turned around with a horrible look and said, "Last year you were running around with a goat and now you want to look like her. She was born beautiful and she is a true lady, a bit of a bitch sometimes but a true woman in every way, you look more masculine than feminine." I felt bad and stuck up for her and said, "If she grew her hair a little, she would look beautiful". She went home very sad while Leo and I went for dinner.

When we returned home that night he said "Min, I want to put a stripping pole in the bedroom. I will pay for it". He had caught me off guard so I said "Ok, no problem." A week later a stripping pole was fitted in my bedroom and I actually started exercising with it.

Milly called me up one day and asked me the directions to an address. I asked her why she was going there and she responded that she had to meet a woman there. She wanted to talk to me. I got a little suspicious and told her I would pick her up after work and take her to meet the woman. I asked Milly why she was meeting this woman. She told me, "I work with her husband and apparently, she wants to kill me. Please Bella, if you don't hear from me in an hour, please call the police. Promise me you won't tell Leo." I said to Milly, "If you aren't out in an hour, I will come looking for you." Milly went into the coffee shop and I sat in the car.

Milly walked into the coffee shop and sat down at the table where a woman named Lidia was already sitting. Lidia was the wife of another dealer. Milly was behind Leo's crops and she was in it all for herself. She spoke to Lidia for a good hour. I decided to go into the coffee shop, so I put on a hat and sunglasses. I could see the two ladies were still in there. They were speaking Albanian. I couldn't make out what they were saying. I sat down at a nearby table and ordered coffee trying not to look conspicuous. Sneakily, I started filming them to have proof that the two women were together. I zoomed into the video and noticed that the other woman had a gun in her handbag. When they finished their coffee Milly came up to me looking very scared and confused. Lidia was behind her and she asked me who I was. I said I am Leo's wife. Lidia said that Milly was going for a drive with her. Milly looked very scared and I could tell that something wasn't right. I quickly replied that she isn't going anywhere as Leo has been looking for her all day and she has unfinished business to attend to.

Milly and I hurriedly left the cafe with our hearts in our mouths. Lidia didn't follow us. Milly proceeded to tell me that Lidia had a gun and she was going to put her into her car boot and drive her into the hills and shoot her. I said, "I hope you learned your lesson and would stay away from her husband." Milly then confessed to me that she was the one who had arranged to steal Leo's marijuana crop. Milly had double-crossed Leo. Actually, he had promised to give her half the money but instead he had not given her anything. I said, "How could you do that to Leo, he has been so good to you?" She responded "I don't care about anyone; my family doesn't have a house or food on the table. They don't know where their next meal is coming from or even if it is coming. It is my job to provide for them." I started feeling sorry for Milly, but she was the worst seed you could come across. It was a shock for me to find out that she was a thief and that too one of the worst kinds you could meet.

When we arrived back at my house Leo had still not come home so I sat her down and asked her, "Tell me what the hell is going on with you? How do you get yourself into these situations? I don't want to frighten you but if you don't stop stabbing them in the back and chasing the dollar sooner or later they will kill you." Milly then started telling me that when she first came to Australia she had met two Albanian brothers. They paid her to look after a crop of marijuana in a house. She received money for the first crop which she sent home to her parents as they were homeless and had no food. The second crop was even larger. Milly recounted that "One night I was watching the news on a little TV I had on the floor and I saw that the police had raided a house. It was like a scene from the movies. I panicked and when the two brothers arrived to have a look at the crop, I told them that I wanted out. We ended up in an argument and one of the brothers pulled a knife and stabbed me three times in the leg. I screamed because of the pain and the brothers fled. The neighbour heard me screaming and she called the police. I got arrested and spent a month in jail. I never gave out the names of the brothers to the police".

She continued, "The policeman who was looking after my case was really nice and found me a room in a share house. Bella, I never found any peace here in Australia. I kept jumping from the boiling pot into the frying pan. It wasn't until recently that the brothers got caught growing marijuana. They both received an 11-year sentence each. Once they complete their sentence they will be deported back to Albania." Milly then proceeded to tell me that she met Leo and his brother through another Albanian mob. The mob treated her like one of their own as she was always loyal and fearless. Leo's older brother broke her when he raped her. She couldn't get past this and started seeing things in a different light. In the end, it was Milly who brought these Albanian members to their knees. She worked endlessly with the police to catch these men out. The men had no idea who was talking to the police. In the end, justice was served.

A few months later Milly stopped paying the rent telling everyone that her mother was dying of cancer and she needed money to go back to Albania to see her. Milly's mother wasn't sick, there was nothing wrong with her. Milly went back home to marry her cousin so she could bring him to Australia as well and so they could wheel and deal together. From what I heard he was a very bad man. Leo didn't want anything more to do with them.

Two years later, I bumped into Milly at a shopping centre and she mentioned that Lidia and her husband had divorced. Her ex-husband had gone back to Albania and married someone else. Karma came to Lidia as she ended up in jail and was out on bail with an ankle bracelet.

At that time Leo was renting a huge house for $300 per week. Leo had marijuana plants growing throughout the house. He slept there every night for about two months and finally, the plants were ready to harvest. One day Leo decided to go and get a haircut and when he returned to the house all the plants were gone. Someone had taken the lot and he never found out who did it, but he knew that it was one of his people. Milly was devastated but Leo found out that his so-called best friend was running around behind his back with another Albanian man who had just come out of prison. Milly became a thief not long after being with this man. She called me one day to ask if I could drive her to the other side of town as she didn't know how to get there.

On a Friday night when I returned home from work, Leo asked me to pack his bags as he was going on a business trip for a few days. I pleaded with him to take me as well as I had the weekend off from work. The look on his face was as if I was an undercover policewoman or a criminal. He replied, "Absolutely not" and started shaming me about my age by saying hurtful things like "You are going in a box to the cemetery". I started feeling sorry for myself and tears started flowing down my cheeks. Once again I felt like a knife had stabbed me in the heart. I knew that he was taking cheap shots at me but there was no point in arguing with him. After everything I had done for him and his family, I felt so alone and sad and that I meant so little to him. I have lost count of the number of times I have gone down on my knees apologising for things I hadn't done.

I was so unhappy and sick and tired of his madness. He was out of control. He believed he was above the law and that he was unstoppable. At the same time, my bad habits led me to have a long conversation with a stranger late into the night. I barely recognised the man who stole my heart. I could no longer talk to him unless he wanted something while at the same time,

All in the Name of Love

I knew he was being unfaithful to me. I was wasting away. My love for him was so strong, my empty heart was bleeding and my broken soul was forever asking for his approval. My pain was unbearable, it was like having broken ribs that nobody can see but the pain is unbearable with every breath.

My heart was constantly at war with my emotions and at the same time, I knew my kindness was my strength though he was forever abusing my beautiful brave soul. My faith is so strong that I would make time to help others even if I was struggling with my problems. I guess we will never know when he stopped loving me. Maybe I am not cut out for love and maybe I am meant to walk alone or perhaps it's only in my loneliness that I can love as I do. I would rather spend my days alone, sitting on a bench in the park and listening to the birds twittering. It takes me back to my childhood when I would be sitting on the side of the road catching my breath. I believe in this messy imperfect difficult vision of love that settles for the bland taste of companionship without passion to love or to hurt but that is not true loneliness. But rejection hurts and losing someone hurts. The only thing that covers pain is bravery and never looking back. I have always been afraid of losing him so have always been trying to please everyone around me.

Chapter Twenty

The next morning Leo got out of bed and we had breakfast together. I cooked bacon and poached eggs. As usual, I served his black coffee in one of my Versace cups. He called me over and said, "You know that I love you but you're getting older and you need to stay home and relax". I replied, "If I stay home and relax who is going to pay the bills?" Leo responded "You have plenty of money, stop being so tight." He begged me for ten thousand dollars saying he will pay me back. Leo knew all too well how to get money out of me. I replied, "I will see what I can do". He reached out and grabbed me at the breakfast bar. He kissed me passionately. I used to love this man but now he was just an empty space. All my dreams were drifting away.

Leo had to go to the bathroom, and I saw that he had left his phone on the breakfast bar. It started ringing and I yelled out to him that his phone was ringing. He asked who it was and I replied, "It's your evil brother". I took the phone over to him and of course, I couldn't understand the conversation as they were speaking Albanian. He said, "Bella I have to go, don't let anyone inside the house". He grabbed his luggage, pecked me on the cheek, and said "See ya. I will be back on Monday

All in the Name of Love

afternoon". And as per his custom, whenever he was going he would say "Do you love your gorgeous?' I always smiled and said yes. I asked him if his evil brother was going with him. He said that he was going on his own. As he got into the car I felt as if my heart was skipping a beat, I already felt so lost and I couldn't understand why I was feeling like this.

That afternoon I went for a walk and when I returned I wrote in my journal. Before I knew it, it was bedtime. I slept soundly that night. My phone was ringing and it was 6 am. It was Leo's sister-in-law. I answered the phone and quickly asked her "What's wrong?" I knew there was something not right because she only called when she needed something. She asked me if Leo was home and I said, "Why are you asking me? Has something happened?" "No, no I just wanted to know if my husband was with him." I replied, "No he isn't with him. Leo is away on business. Why don't you call him?" She said she had tried calling but Leo's phone was switched off. I said "I can't help you" and hung up the phone.

I quickly called Milly and asked her if she knew where Leo's evil brother was and that his wife was looking for him. Milly said Leo and his evil brother were at a brothel last night. I was shocked as Leo had told me that he was going to Melbourne. Milly said, "No, no he is going to Mildura this morning but will be back on Sunday afternoon." I asked her if she knew why he was going to Mildura. She said she didn't want to hurt me, but Leo had met someone online and was spending the weekend with her. I said, "Ok, no problem, thanks". The voices started in my head, "Report him to the police. He is nothing but a low-life who is just using and abusing me. I hope he will rot in hell for all I care." I realised that it was impossible for him to be honest. He was never happy no matter what, whether it was searching for his next sexual conquest or drugs. Little did he know that bad karma was waiting for him around the corner.

Perhaps he thought if he gave more love he would get more in return. Maybe he thought he would be a better gangster by getting others to love him. He was using so many people to fulfill his dreams and he couldn't care less who he trampled over along the way. He didn't care about anyone. Slowly, Leo was destroying my soul. How many tears had I cried over him or how many times I had apologised for things I never did or said. I used to think the worst thing was to be alone for the rest of my life. But I felt like a fool as no one could love him as I did. I said to myself, "Stop expecting loyalty from people who can't even give you honesty."

A few hours later Milly rang me and asked if I would like to catch up with her at the beach. She said please Bella. I asked her if everything was ok. She said, "You need to know about Leo." I thought to myself, "What has he done now?" Milly wasn't at the beach when I arrived. So I went up to the bar and ordered myself a double margarita. Finally, she arrived and I was very curious to know what she had to tell me. It just took a fake smile to hide my injured soul. She didn't know how broken I was.

Milly began to tell me how Leo and she were working one day and Leo's mum rang to let him know that she had found him a beautiful young 18-year-old virgin bride. She was waiting for Leo to get his green card. I asked her how she knew this. Milly replied that she was on the speaker and that is how she heard the whole conversation. He had even handed Milly the phone so she could speak to his mum. His mother asked me if I knew this girl and I told her that back home she lived down the road from her house. I stayed very calm and replied, "I am not surprised but anyway I wish her all the best. She would need it.

I asked Milly if she knew why Leo had gone to Mildura instead of Melbourne. She replied yes and I asked her to tell me. Milly told me, "Leo met someone online and he thinks that he is in love again. He is spending the weekend with her." So I said to her, "It takes a lot for me to give up on someone so where the hell did he spend Friday night as Leo and his evil brother had gone to Mildura on Friday morning and they spent their time in a brothel." She said, "Don't worry he is not going to leave you for her." I replied, "Yeah, lucky fucking me. Not that I want you to know the truth that I was used and abused and still stayed. Just know that I did everything I could for that family to keep him safe." Milly became very teary, but I had to choose my words carefully as I didn't trust her. But deep down in my heart I knew she was telling me the truth but she had crushed my heart.

I picked up my big Versace sunglasses. I looked like an Albanian gangster's wife but the job had gone wrong. I ordered a shot of tequila for myself and then went back home. For the first time, I reached home and took a good look at myself. I knew that my wings were broken and that my face was covered with dirt, dust, and pollution. He had tried to destroy me and bring me down to his level. But I lived, I have been hurt but I am alive. I am human, I am not perfect, but I fell in love. The truth is that I can't let him get away with this. I don't have the strength so a time will come when I would have to lay it down as the past and hold him accountable for all the things that he had done to me. It was a chapter of my life that I had to let go. I was very grateful to Milly for confiding in me. I was ready to do everything in my power to destroy him to the point that he won't know what hit him.

I remember Leo always saying don't ring me, so I did just that. I tried calling and texting him but of course, there was no reply. I texted "I hope you are ok and not just avoiding me as I thought a professional man like you would show me some decency. I respect that you are busy, however, it takes only a couple of seconds to reply to my messages. Stay safe". A couple of hours went by and there was nothing, no response. I was so angry. I am sure he would answer quickly to a stranger. I decided to calm my mind. When I think back to when I first met Leo, he was the kindest person that had ever entered my life. He made me see the sun when everyone else saw clouds. He made me believe that anything was possible in this life.

From that day on I lived my life. I would go out so I could catch him out in public. Finally, luck was with me when he had an interview with the Immigration department and they detained him. Within two weeks he was moved to Christmas Island. The day they detained him I went to a hotel and bought myself a scotch and coke to celebrate that I was free. I had an angel watching over me. But then his brother started harassing me to try and get him back from Christmas Island. He wanted me to hire lawyers and send him money. Leo was released six months later. He rang me the day before he landed asking if I could pick him up from the detention centre. When I returned his call, he never answered.

I called his brother and he told me that he had already picked him up and the whole family had had lunch at a fancy restaurant to celebrate his return. I asked his brother if I could speak to Leo and he agreed but all Leo was interested in talking about was when he could come back home. Two months later he was at my door, I felt my mouth drop to my chest. He told me he loved me and wanted to move back in. He pushed open the door and came in as if everything was ok. I was badly shaken. A week later I booked myself a trip overseas and left, not wanting to return as I feared for my life.

I went to Europe where I took time to reflect and break out of my emotional prison. My mind could be either a palace or an emotional prison. I had to decide whether to stay in prison or escape. I decided to have no contact with anyone that knew him. While I was in Italy my brother-in-law who lived there, passed away. Upon my arrival back home, my family informed me that Leo had gone to give his condolences at their home and to be careful as they believed that he was doing whatever he could to stay in the family. I asked my sister why she would let him in the door when all he did was criticize me, be it a spoken word or the colour of my hair or what I wore, or anything else he could pick on unless you were his kind. When I came home my thoughts were filled with what if he came here, what would he do to me? I was very emotional and then I laughed and thought what am I doing to myself?

As my day went along, I decided to go to the beach. As I got into the car around 3 pm, I was listening to the radio and there was a news flash. It announced that a car travelling towards the Barossa Valley collided with a truck and two men were critical. I remember the day very clearly as it was a beautiful sunny 27-degree day. The car was travelling along the stretch of road with vineyards along both sides and picturesque scenery. How could such a tragedy occur? The driver of the 4-wheel drive lost control due to a cigarette dropping at his feet. As I was listening my thoughts went to the poor man's family as they said they may not make it. The occupants of the car were transported to a hospital by helicopter.

I stopped to buy takeaway for dinner as I was not expecting Leo to be home until Monday morning. I ate my dinner around 8 pm. I put on a DVD as I began to relax. Suddenly, there was a knock at my door and I thought to myself "Who could that be?" I went to answer the door and there were two police officers on my doorstep. They asked me if they could come in. My thoughts went straight to my house being raided instead I was asked to sit down. They proceeded to tell me that someone who lived at my address was involved in a car accident and the doctors didn't believe he would make it through the night. I replied, "No one by that name lives here". So they showed me a photo of his licence. It was my address and it was Leo. I didn't even cry, I was okay. I informed them that his name was Leo.

All in the Name of Love

The officers told me where Leo was. I got myself ready and called a taxi to go straight to the hospital.

Leo was critical and had been placed in an induced coma. His evil brother was in a coma for seven days and finally came around. They told him the bad news. They found traces of alcohol and drugs in his system and that he was paralysed from the waist down. The car had blown up so who knows what else was in that vehicle.

I spent a couple of nights in the hospital room with Leo, I slept on a hard bed. On the third day, I was pacing the room when there was a knock on his door. There was a young woman with long black hair, possibly in her twenties standing at the door. I asked her to come into the room and she asked me who I was. Not knowing who the woman was I told her I was Leo's friend and then I asked her how she was connected with Leo. She responded that she was his girlfriend. I grabbed my Louis Vuitton handbag and placed my Versace sunglasses on top of my head. I said to this woman, "It was nice meeting you, I will leave him in your capable hands now", and I left. As I was walking along the hospital corridor, I saw two police officers come out of an elevator. They were walking towards Leo's room. I stepped into the elevator and tears streamed down my face, I had such a feeling of relief. Justice was about to be served.

Leo had a pocket full of dreams and nothing was going to stop him from turning those dreams into reality. So, he had set upon a mission to realize that no matter what the consequences or the hurt or the pain or the betrayal he would cause me, he would proceed to fulfill his dreams.

Along the way, Leo may have been able to deceive me, control me and steal from me, not only financially but mentally as well. He defeated me several times, but I never allowed him to control my soul. I may have begged for my freedom and feared for my life due to his threats, but I was now a free strong spirit and all Leo was left with was a pocket full of crumbs.

Six months later I got a message through Facebook from a gentleman named Vittorio, who was trying to impress me. He asked me if I liked younger men and I replied why would you ask me that, I like all men. To which he replied, "I like your look, you are so hot and I love your eyes." He said all the right things but then I told him maybe he should find someone beautiful and young. He replied, "I like older women. They know what they are doing." He started sending me photos of a handsome well-built man, then photos of fancy cars and expensive jewellery. Then he told me that he had so much money but could not find love. I cut him short and said I had to go. We continued to chat for about three weeks. As he had said I was so easy to talk to plus I liked the attention.

One morning I had several messages from him and his last message read, "Where are you, Min? Why aren't you answering me?" When I read that last message, I became nervous and angry as I realised that it was Leo. He was the only one that called me Min. Even though I realized it was him, I replied as if nothing was wrong. I told him that I needed to ask him why he called me Min as

All in the Name of Love

only one person knew me by that name, a nickname my ex-partner had given me and it was our secret and had meant a lot to me at that time. He replied, "I'm sorry Bella. Can I call you Min?" I said no only my ex had the privilege to do so. I sent a photo of Leo and said only this man could call me that. He responded that he is the luckiest man to have had someone like you in his life. He then sent photos of his penis and asked me to score from 1 – 10 and what it looked like and if I liked it. I didn't reply to these comments, but he kept insisting so I played along and told him it was nice and long. So he then sent a photo of the length. I wrote wow that is long, long enough for you to turn around and shove it up your ass and imagine the pleasure you would get because I now know who you are.

It was hard to sleep when my heart was at war with my mind. I often hear his voice calling me Min and the front door opening with Leo calling, "Min I am home".

I hear his voice like the wind whispering, "Min I love you". I thank god that that chapter of my life is behind me.

I would like to thank my beautiful friend Rosie for helping me to complete this book.

Leo had really captured my heart and it took a long time for me to get over him. So, I would not allow myself to get involved with another man for quite some time. I threw myself into my work and any spare time I had I would catch up with friends for dinner. I had re-found myself and felt comfortable and at peace in my own skin. I am not looking for anyone.

My name is Bella and this is my story. Behind closed doors, I drowned my sorrows. I thought of you today, but that isn't unusual. I thought about you yesterday and the day before that too. I think of you in silence. I often hear you calling out my name, "Min I am home". All I have are memories as a keepsake from which I would never part as I have you in my heart to remind me of all the rotten things you have done to me.

www.ingramcontent.com/pod-product-compliance
Lightning Source LLC
Chambersburg PA
CBHW031250290426
44109CB00012B/515